ONLY FLOWERS

COLORING BOOK

70 BEAUTIFUL FLOWER DESIGNS FOR ADULTS RELAXATION

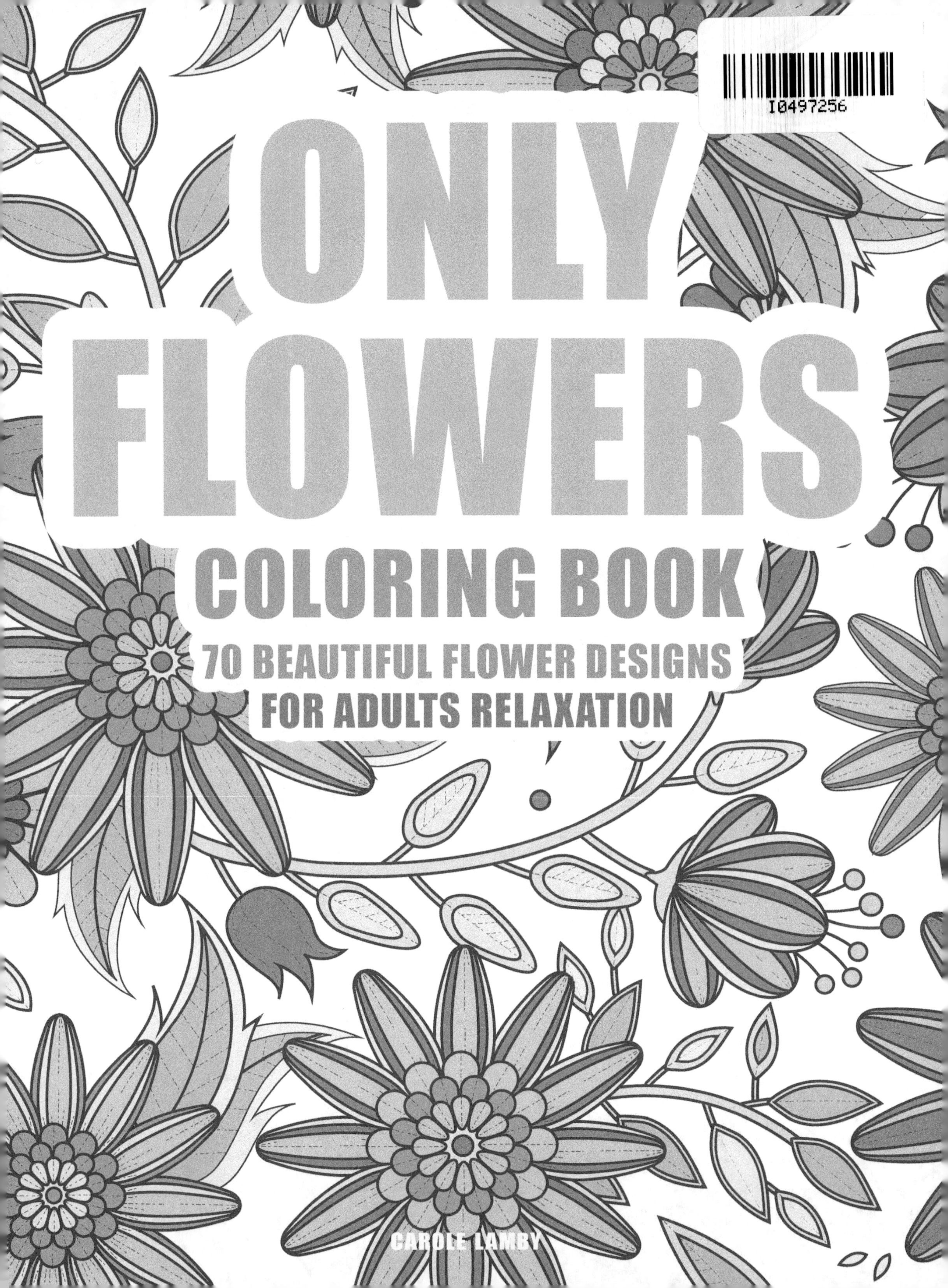

CAROLE LAMBY

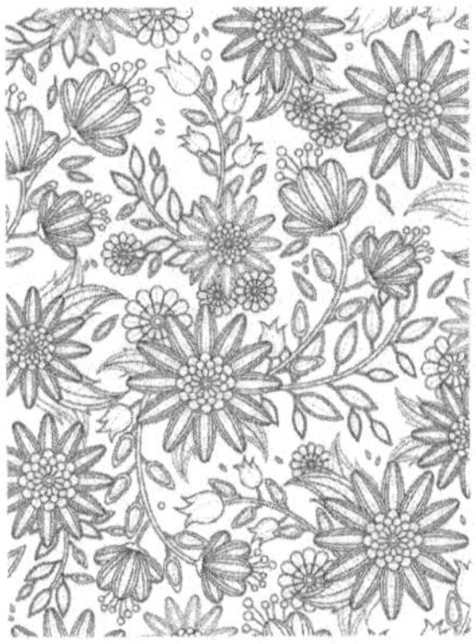
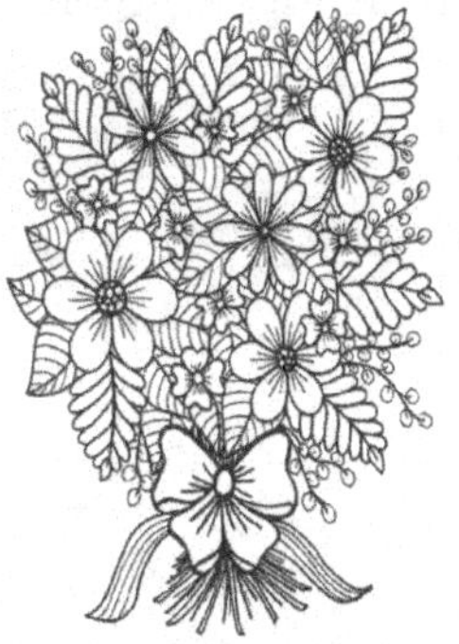
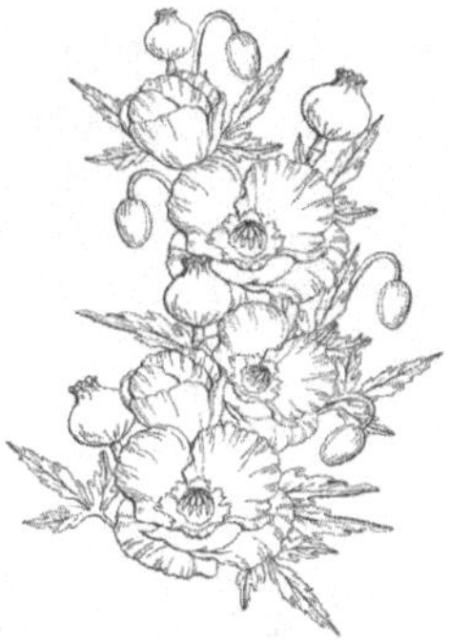
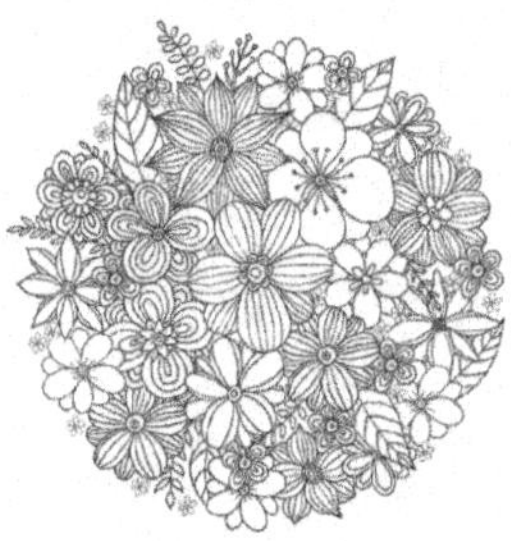
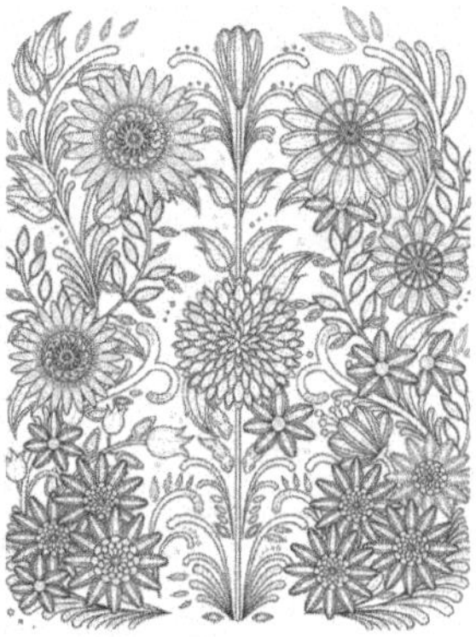

A FEW FLOWER DESIGNS FROM THIS COLORING BOOK

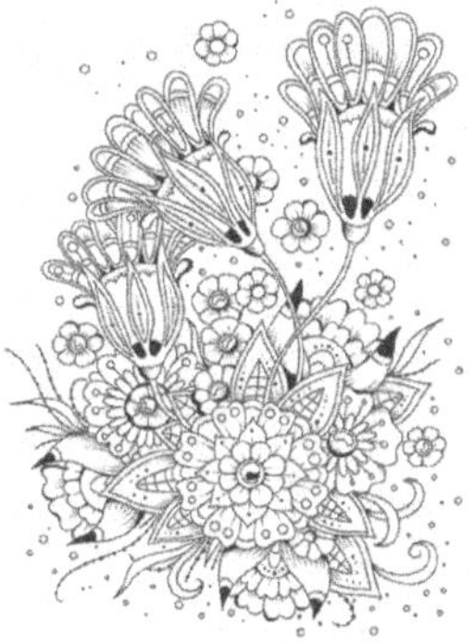
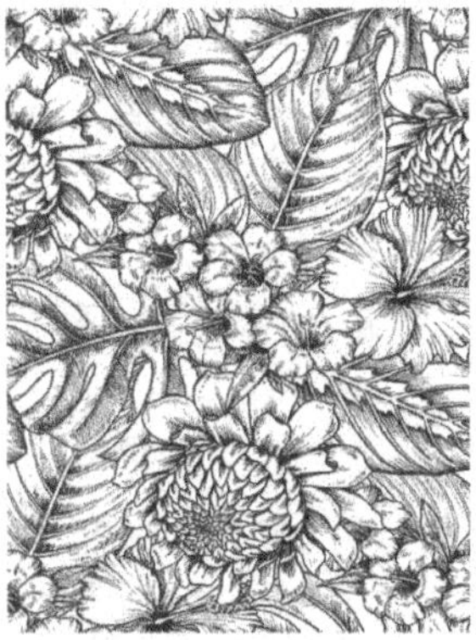
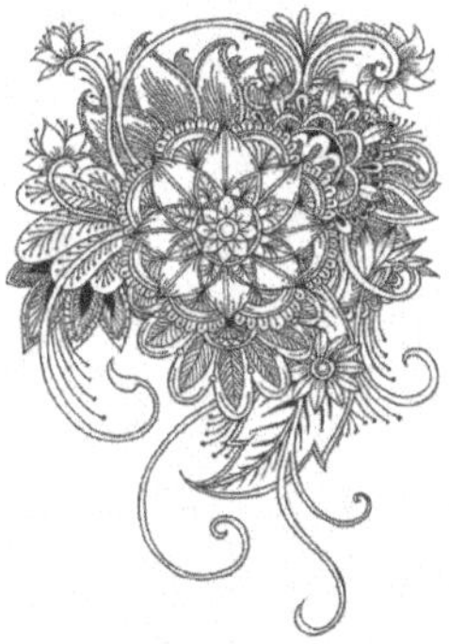
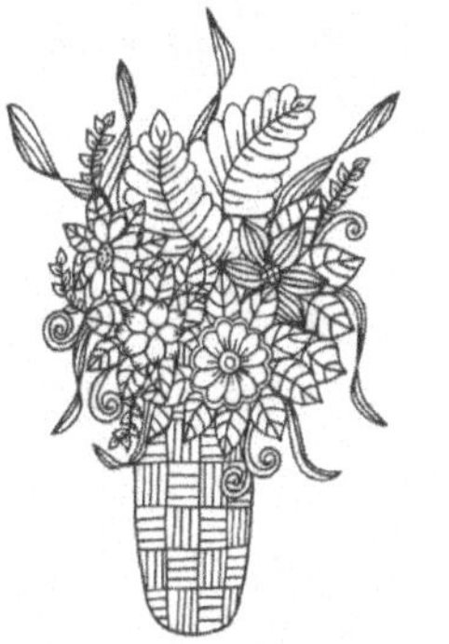
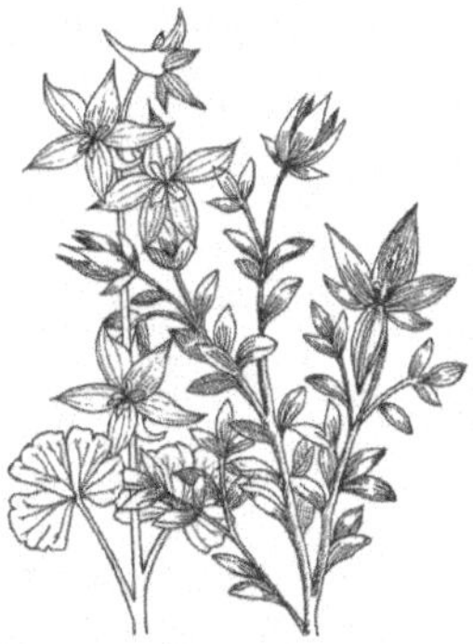
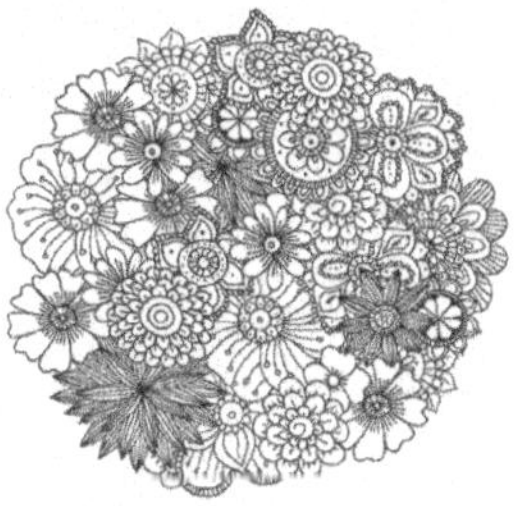
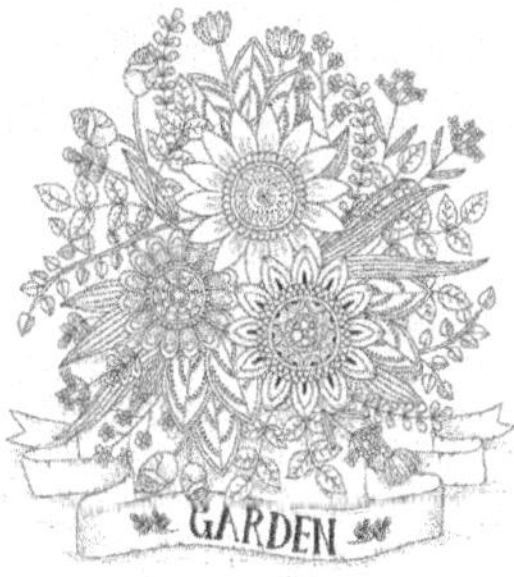
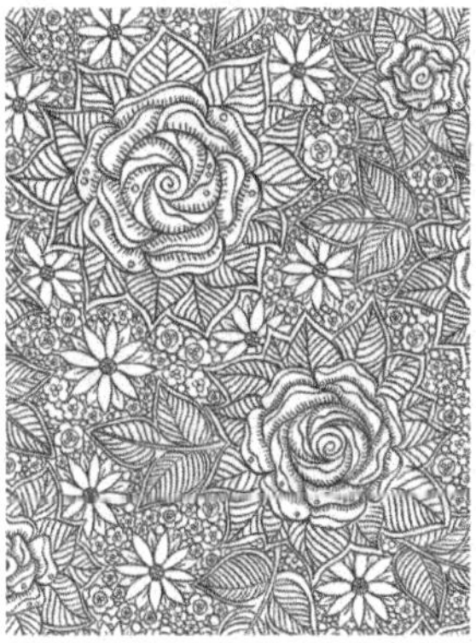
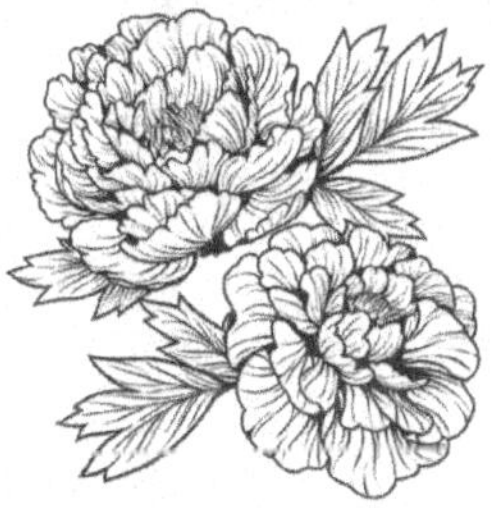
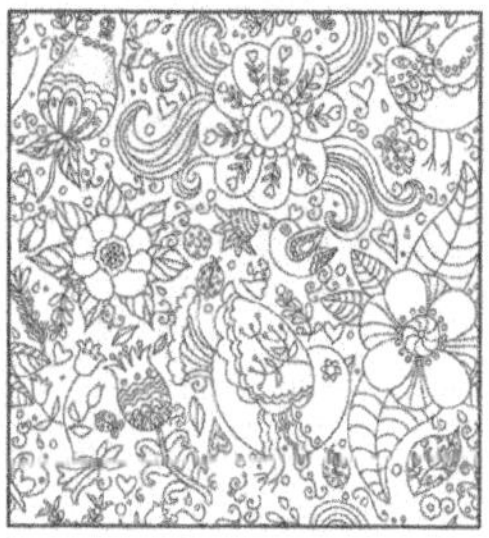
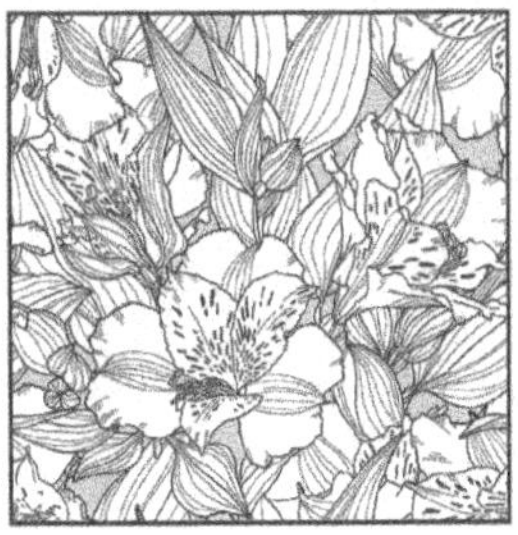
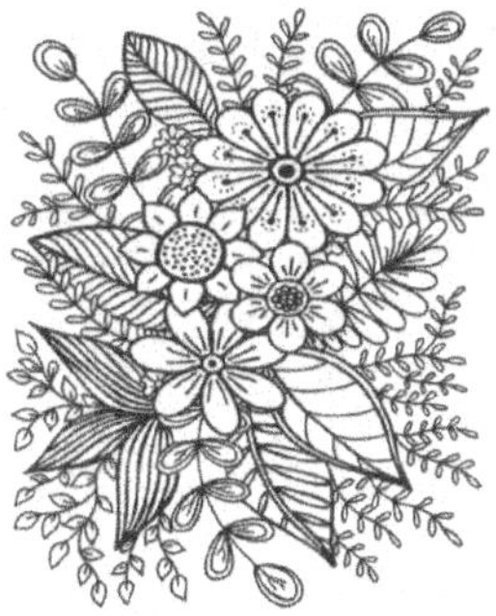
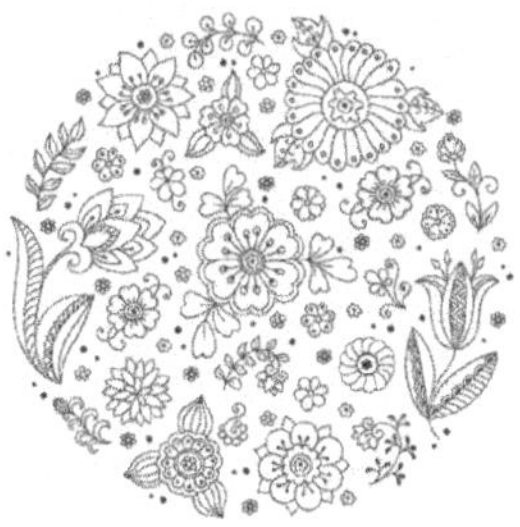
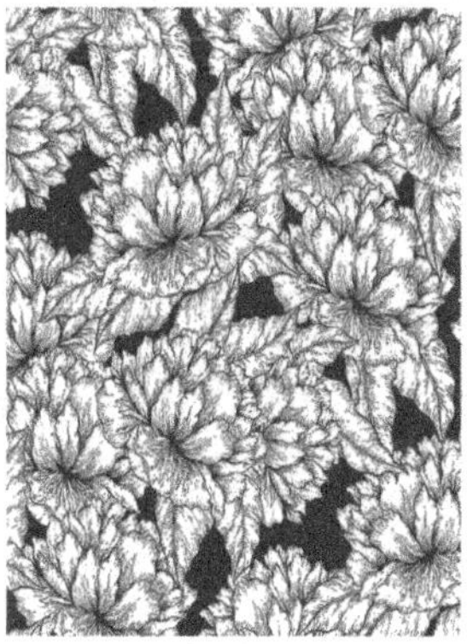
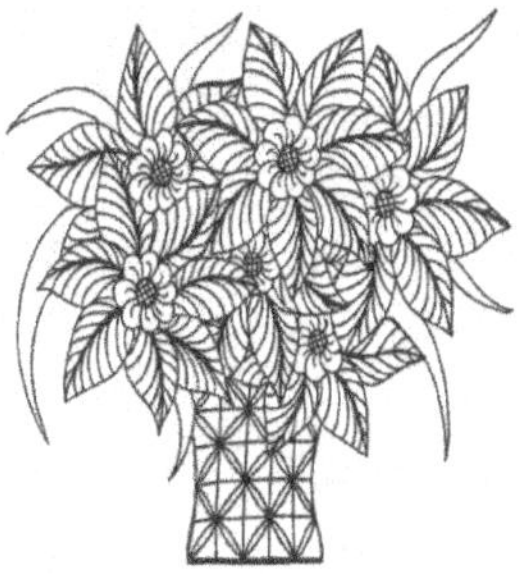
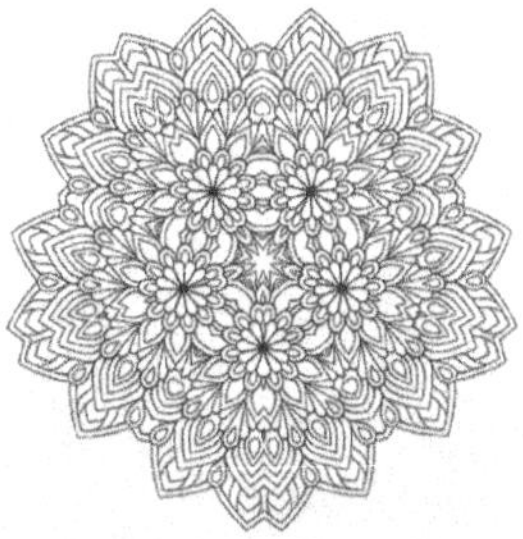
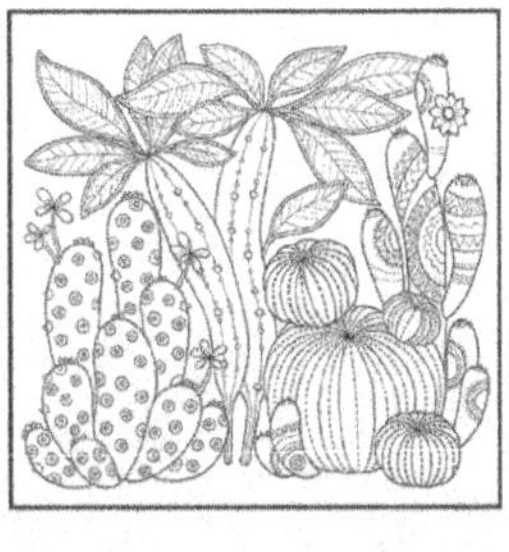
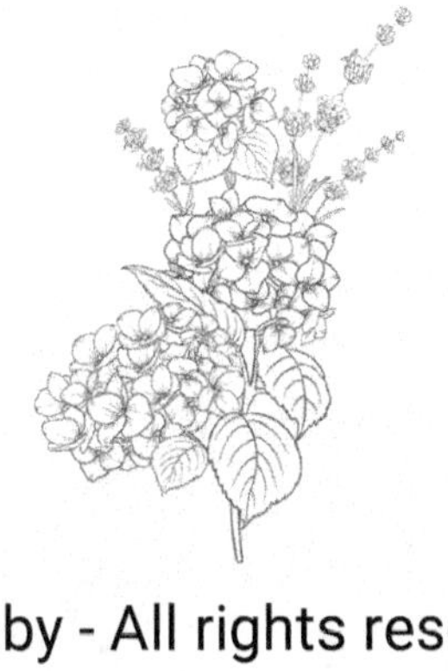
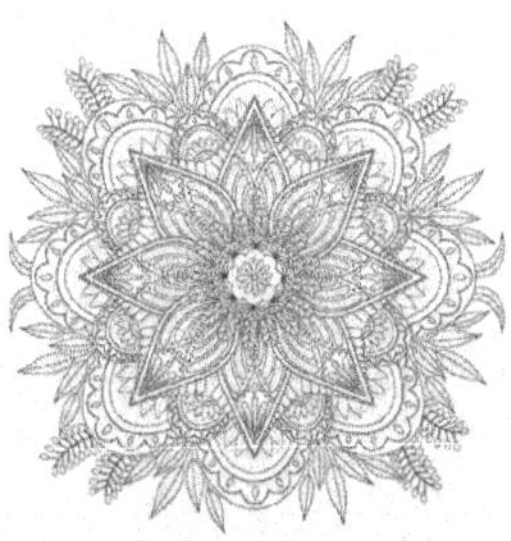
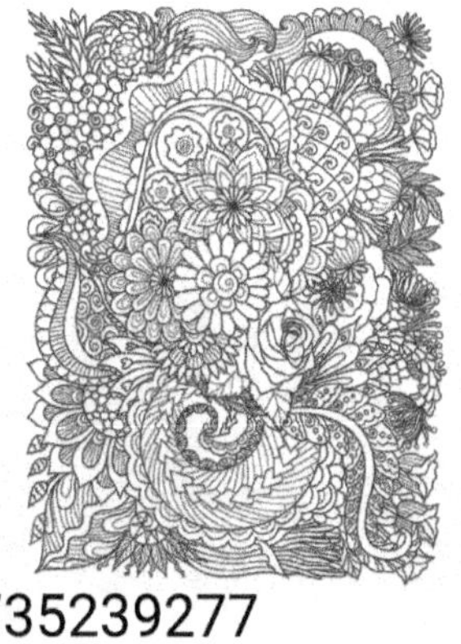

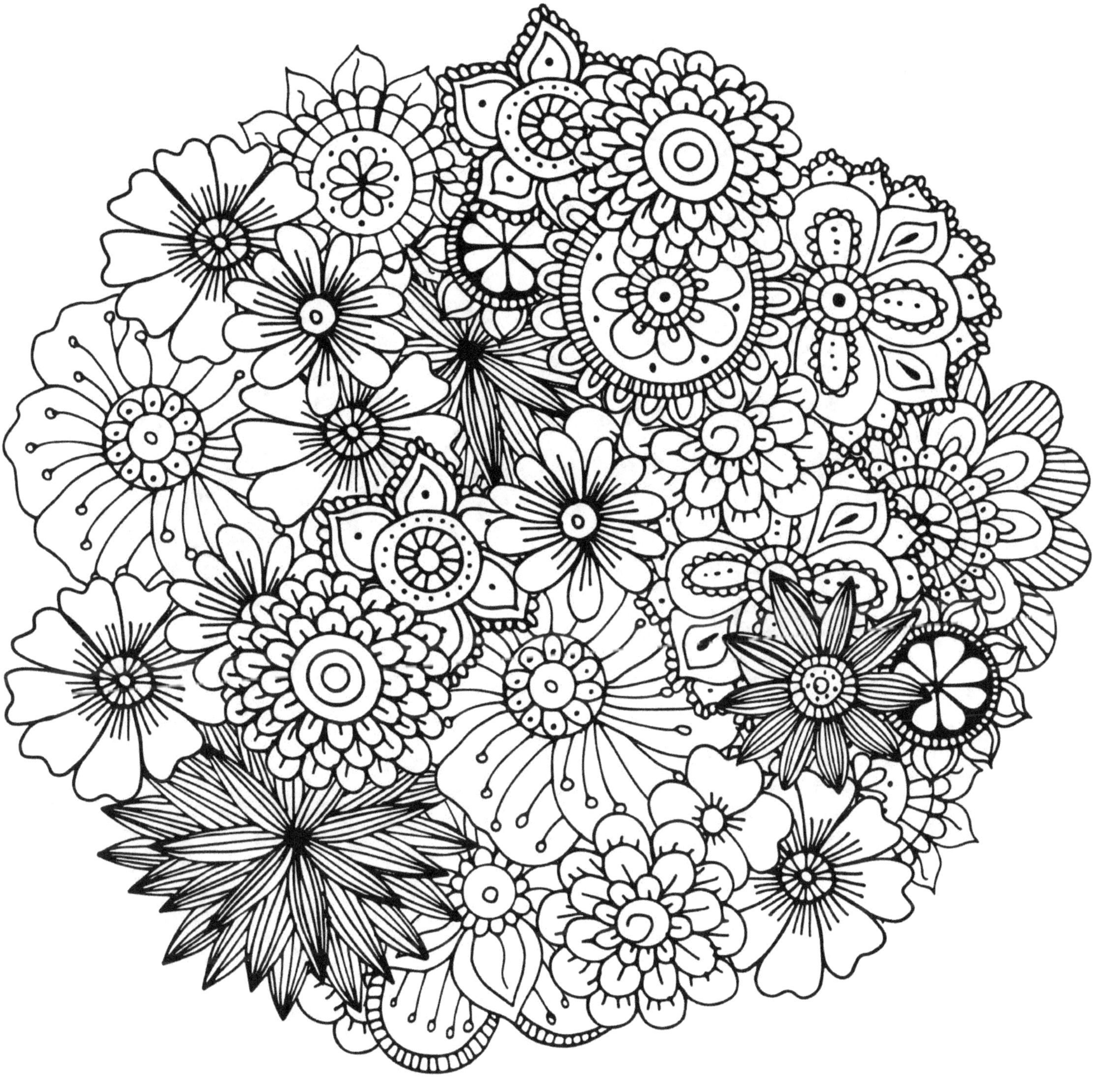

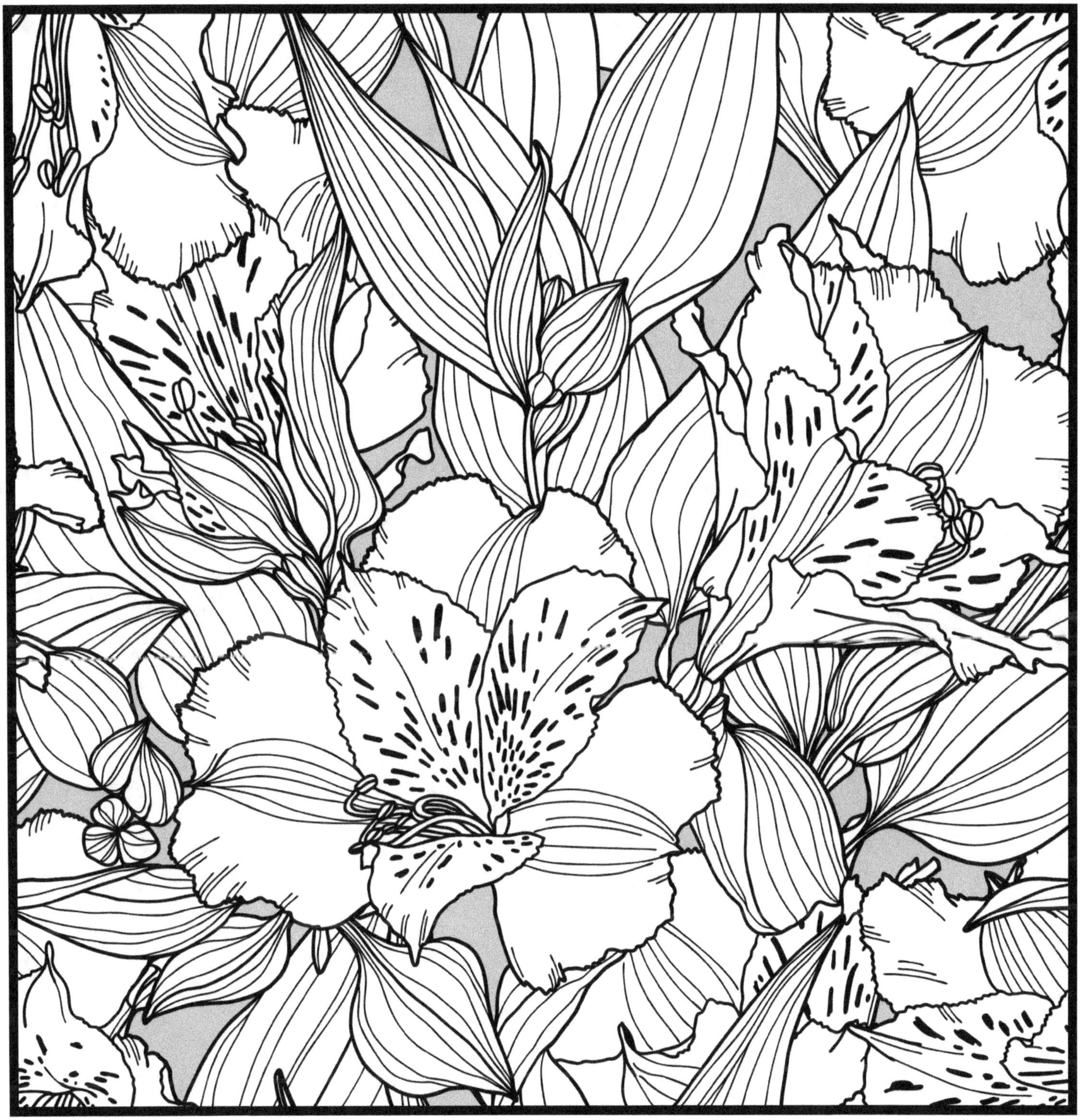

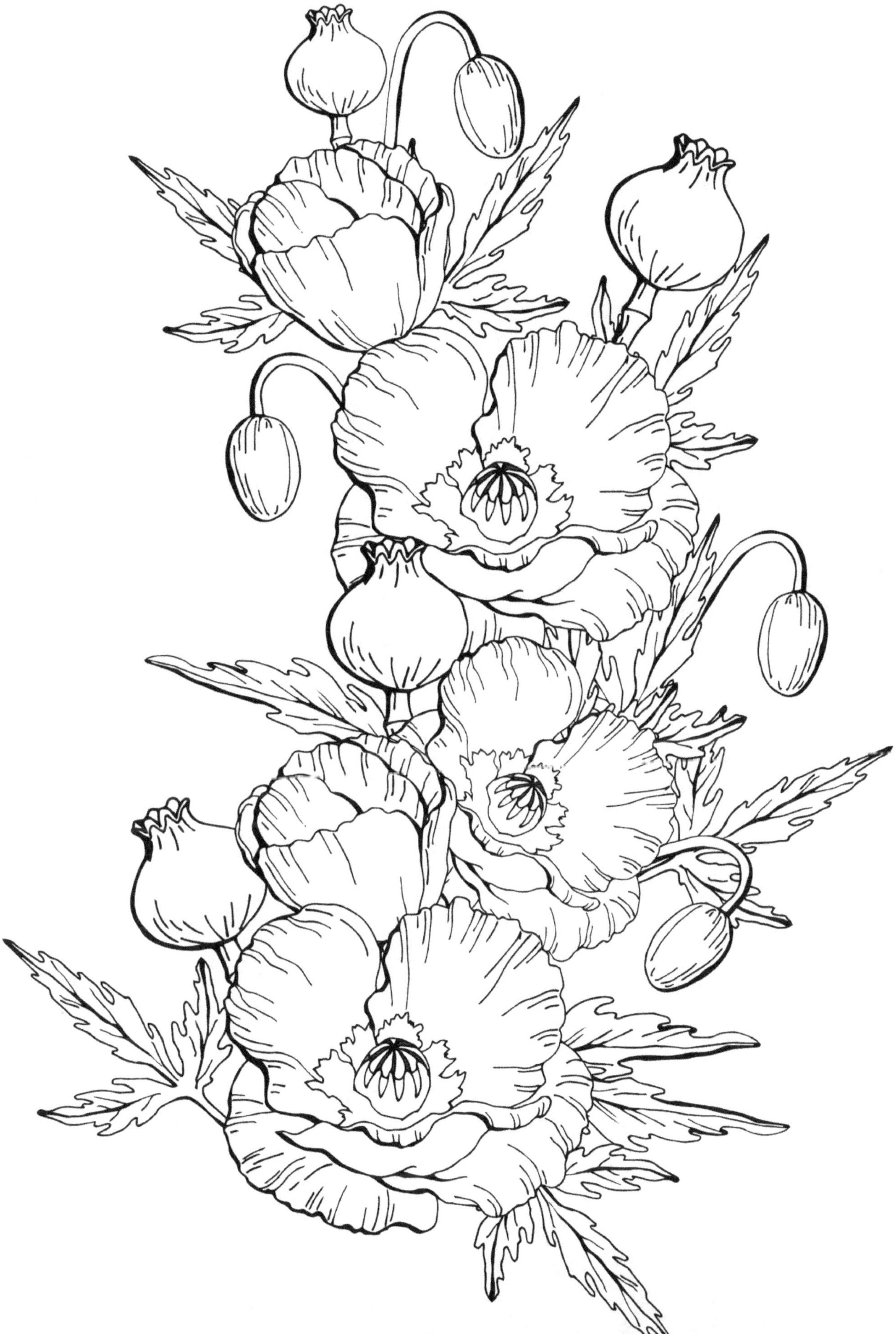

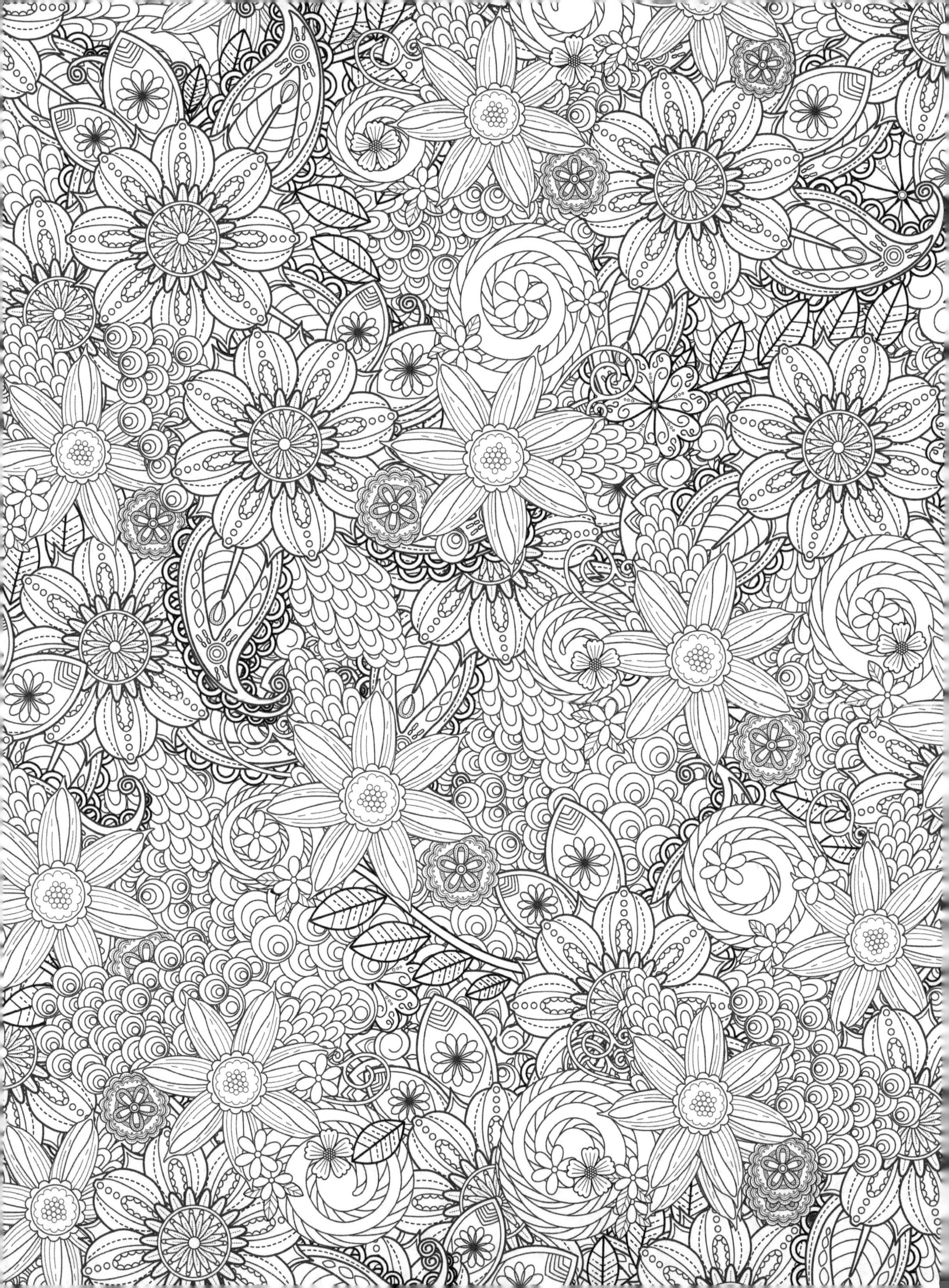

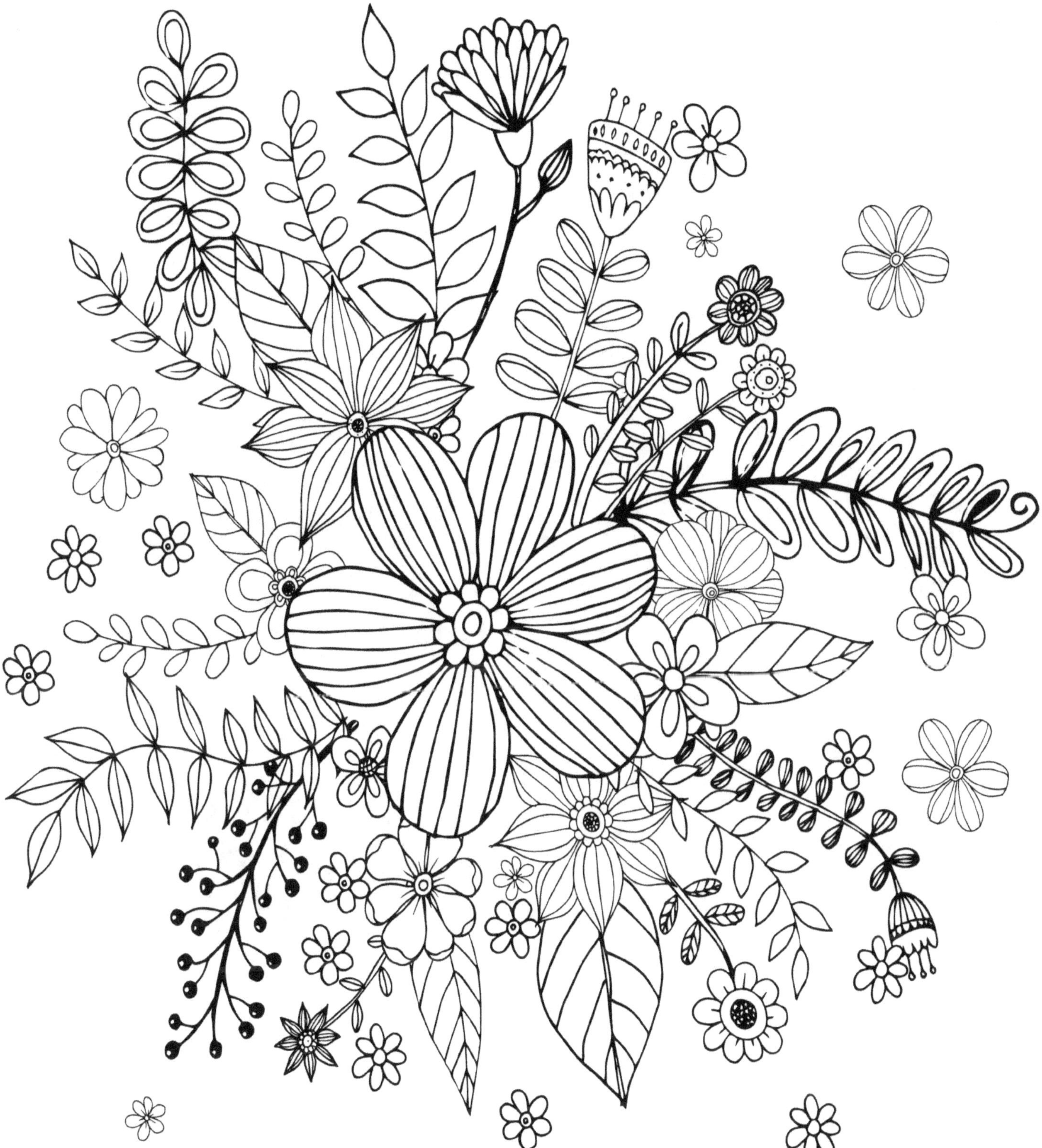

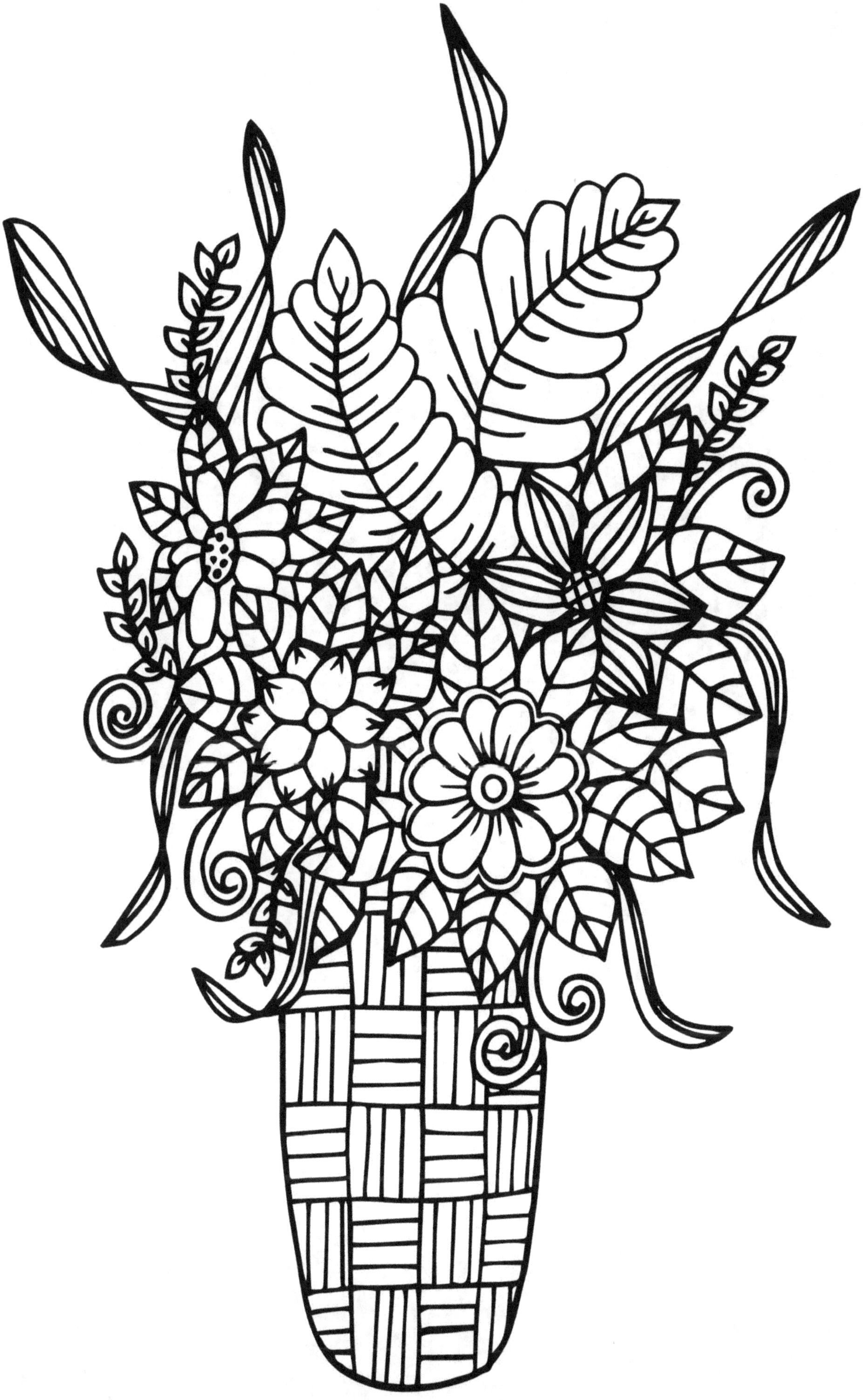

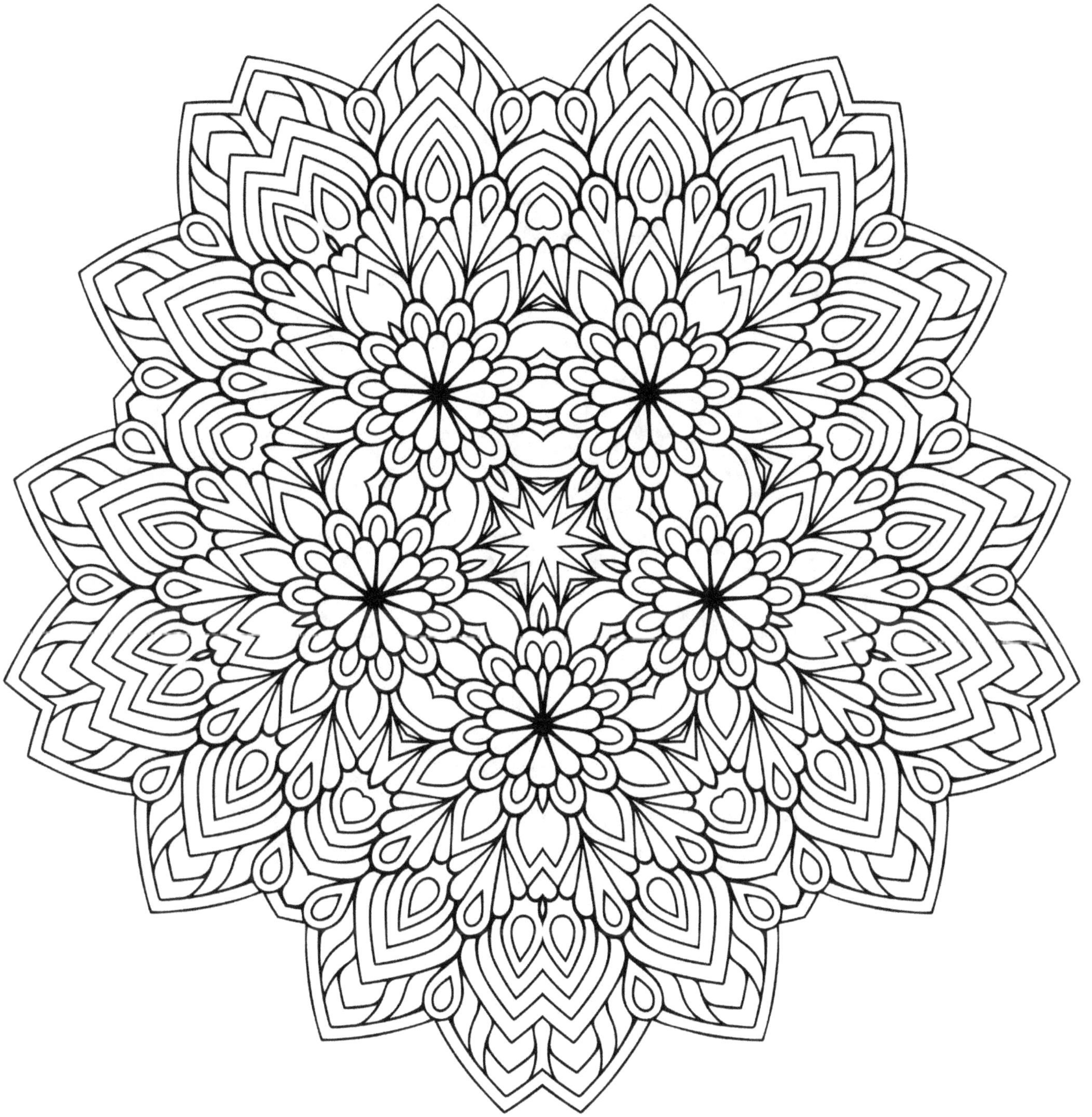

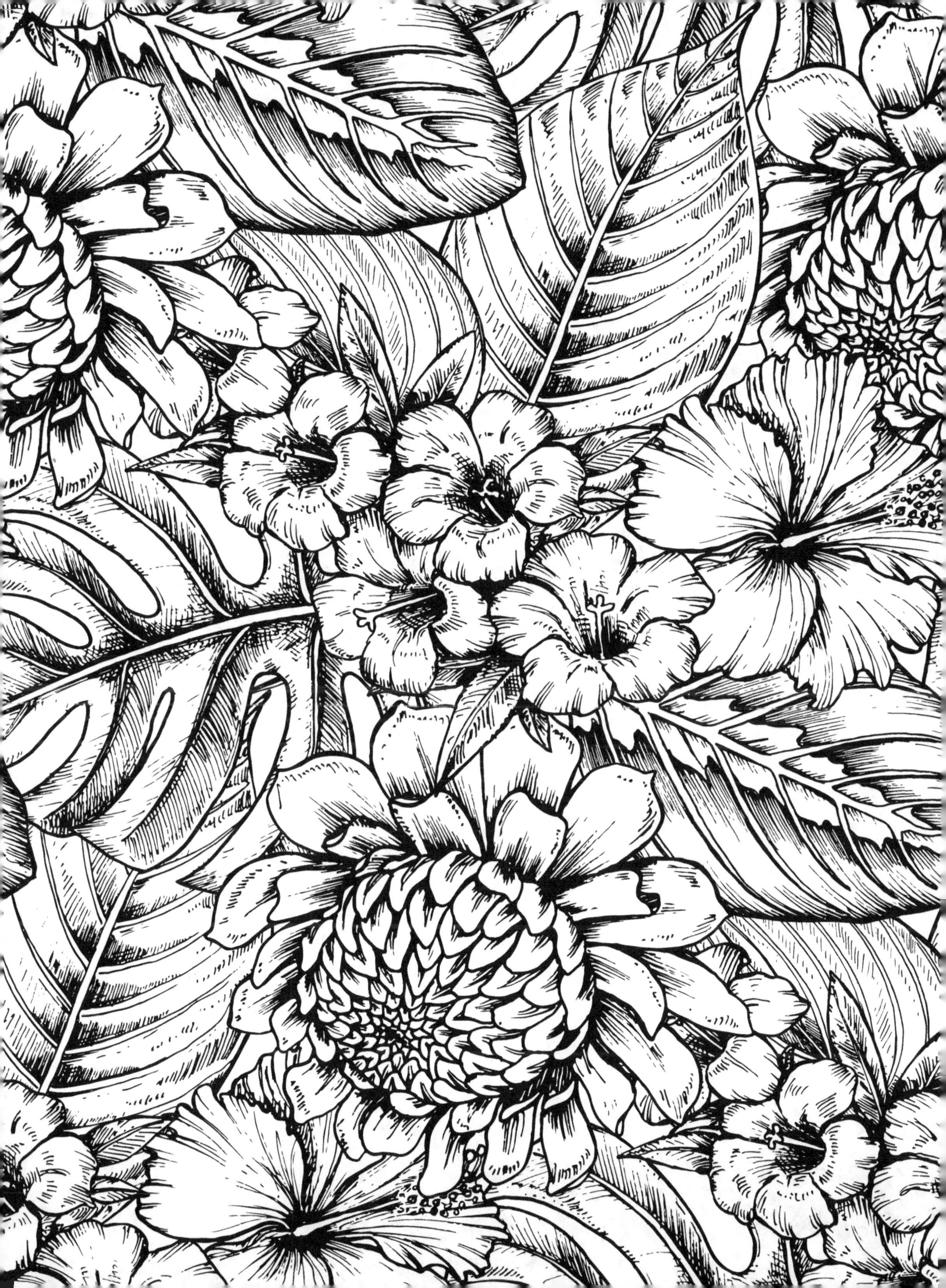

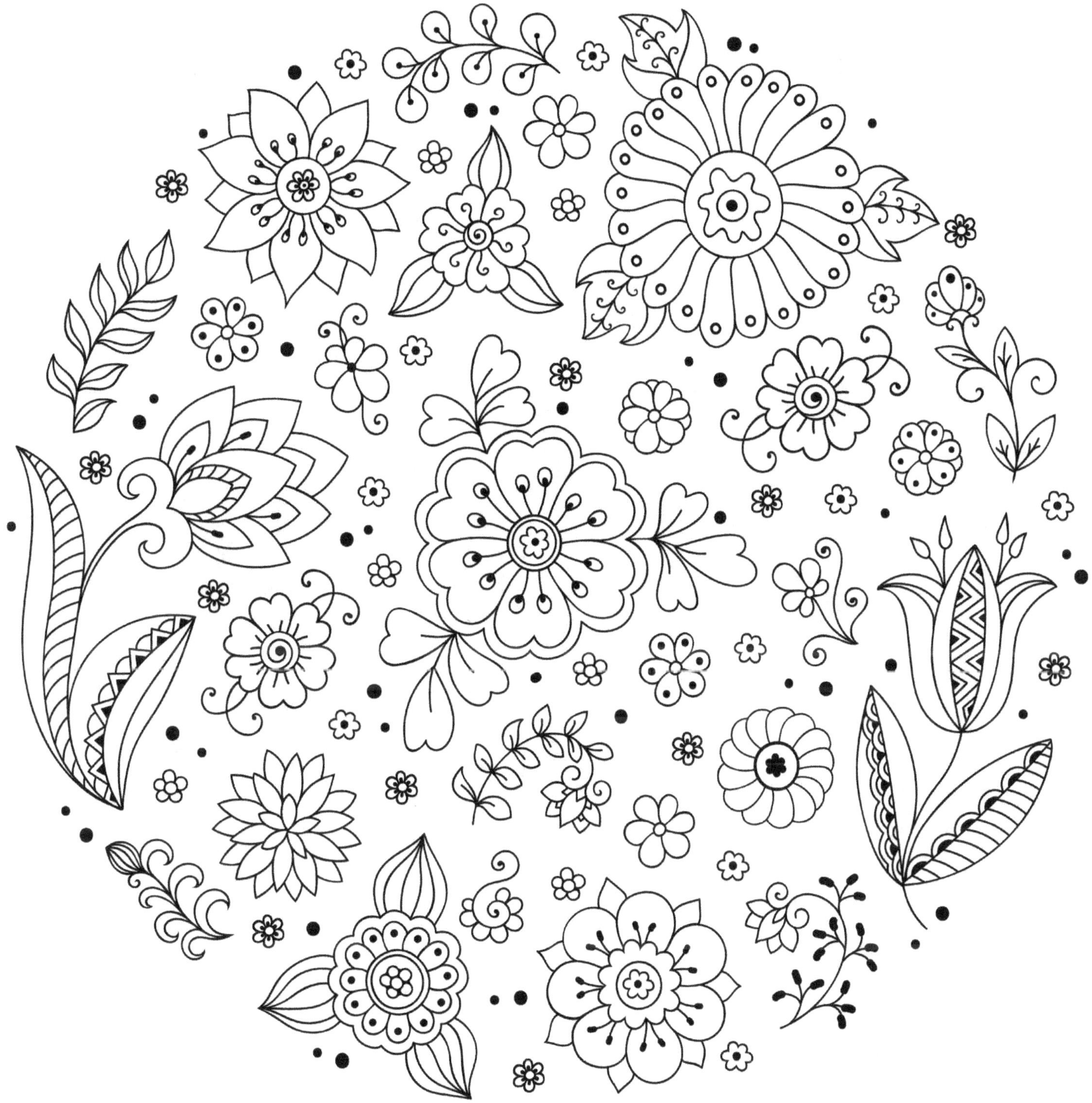

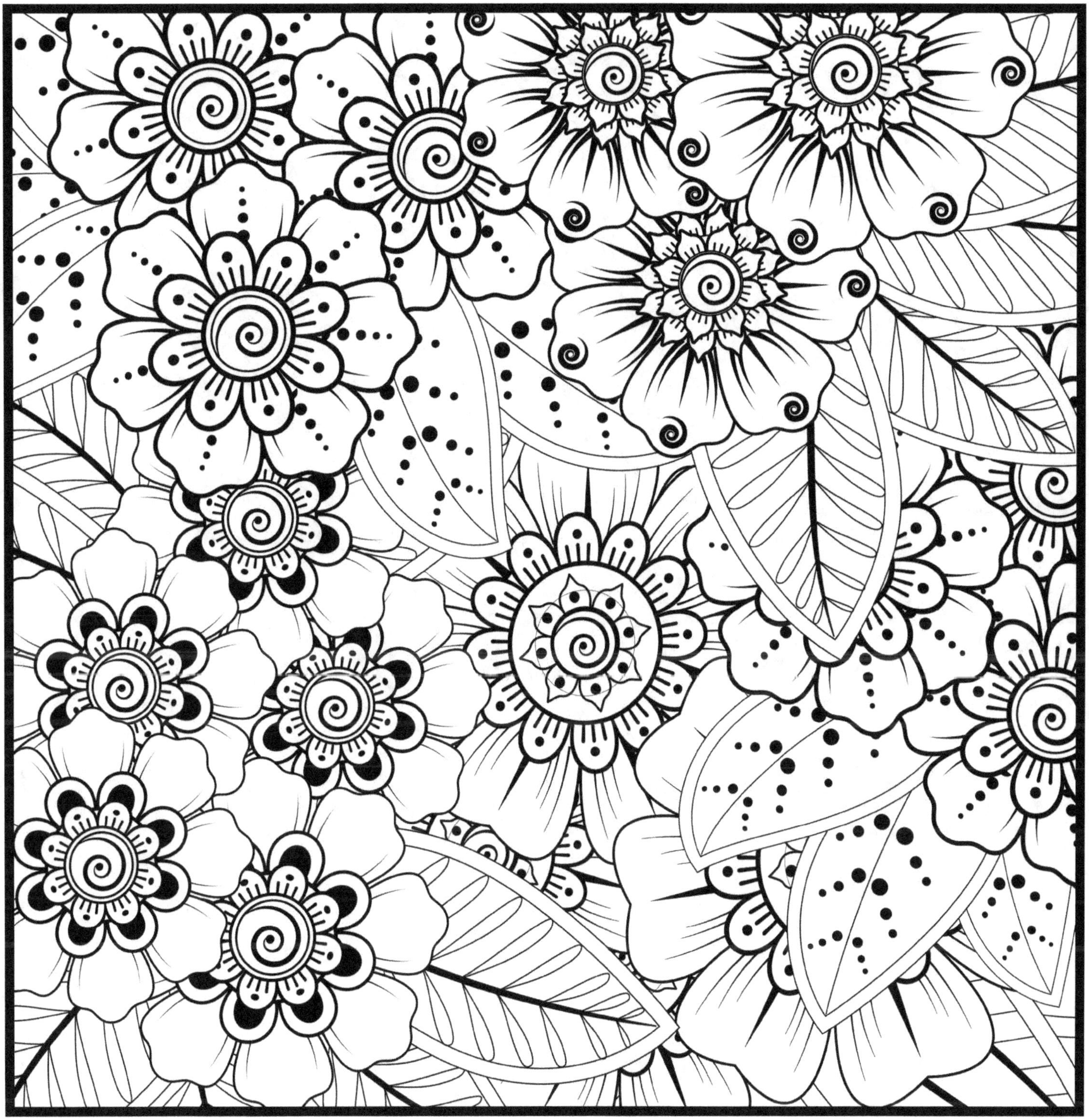

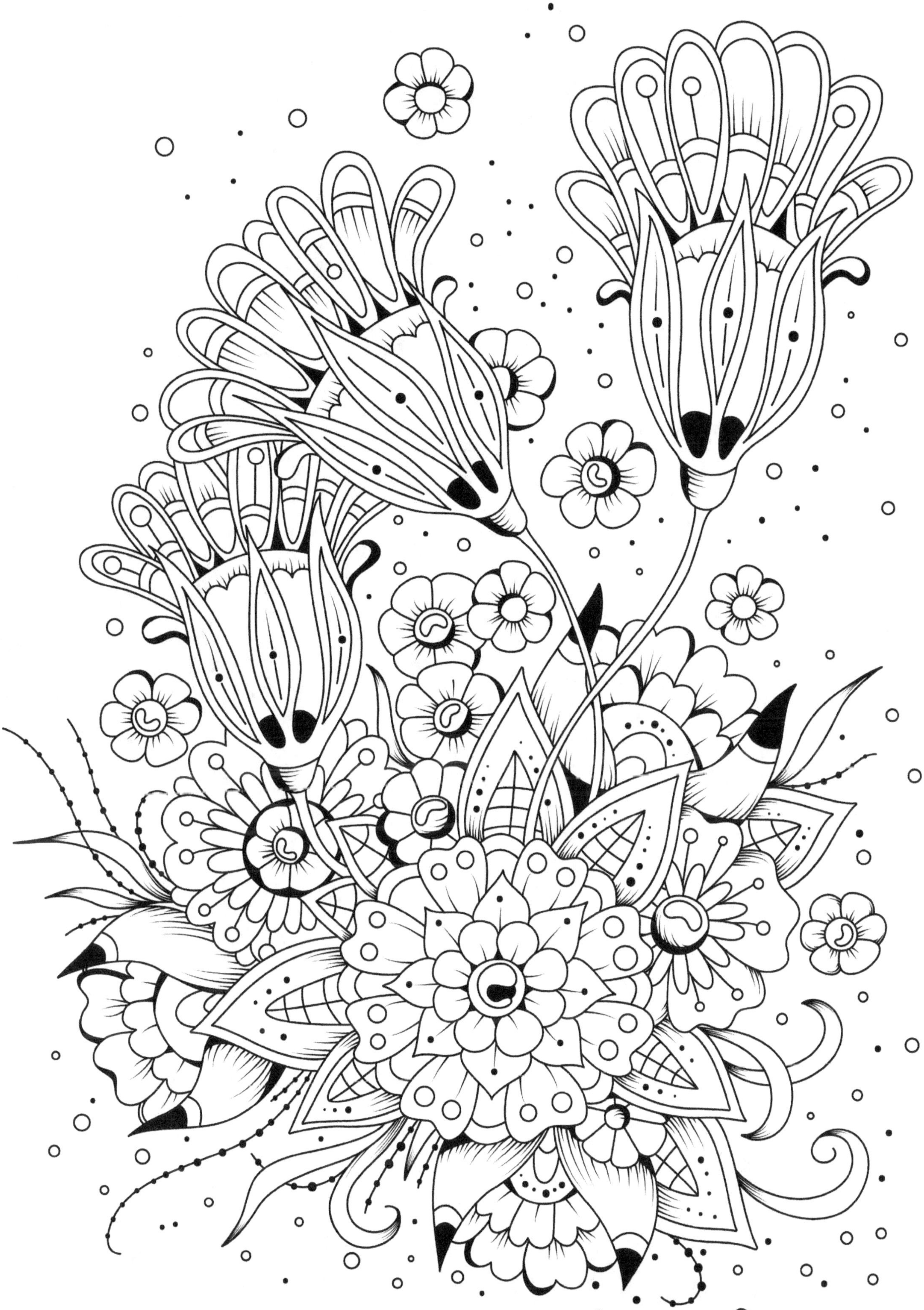

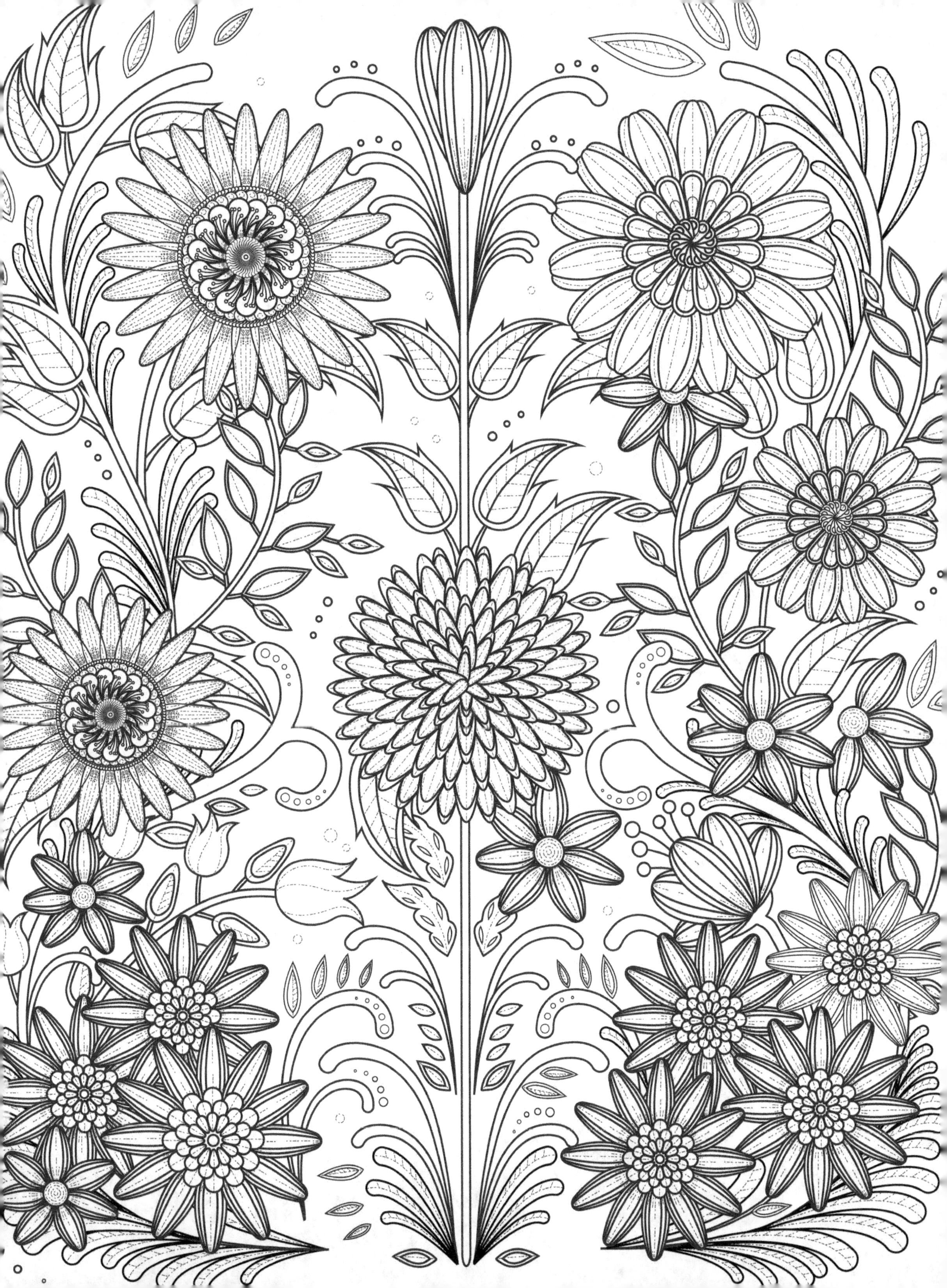

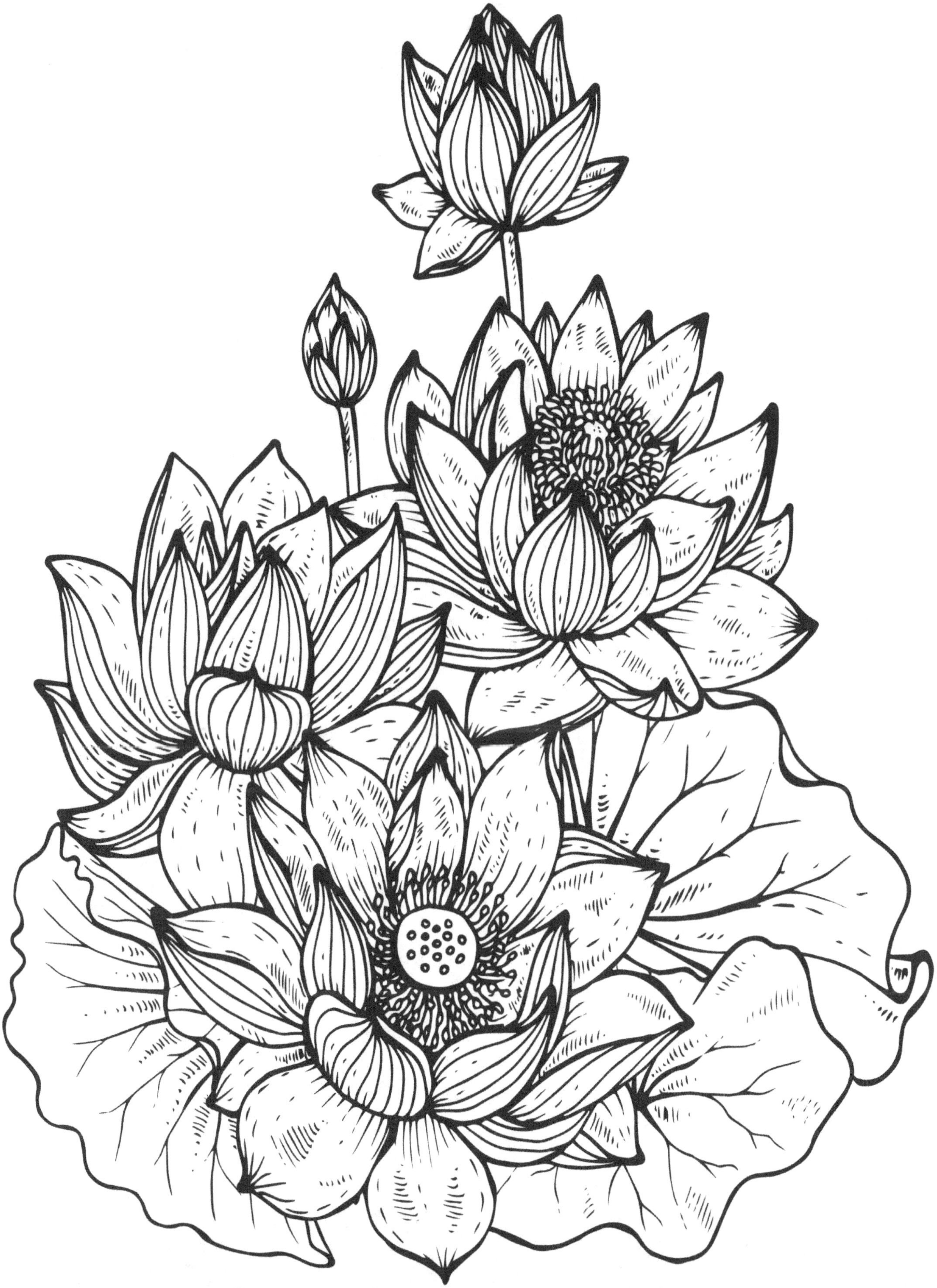

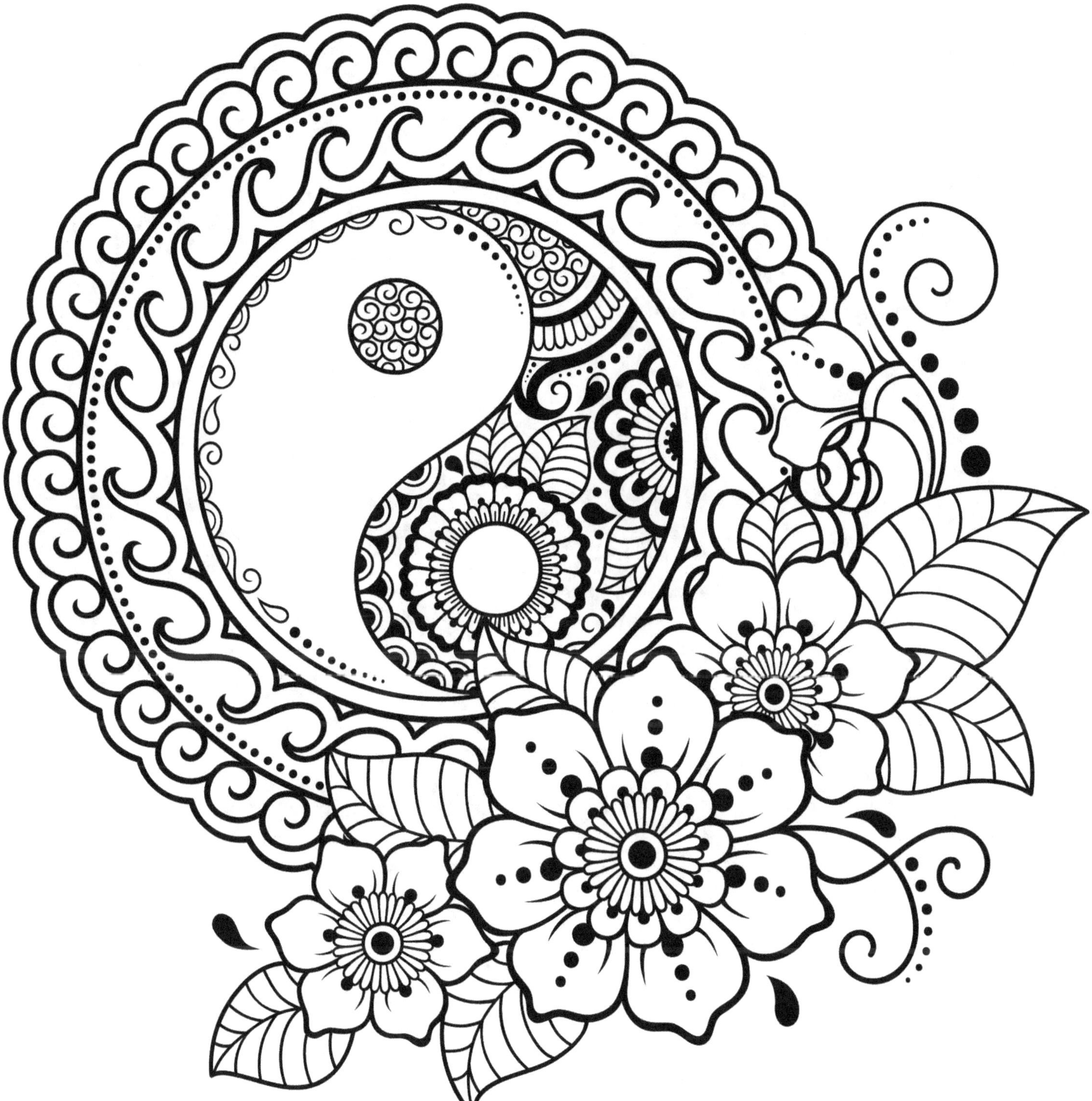

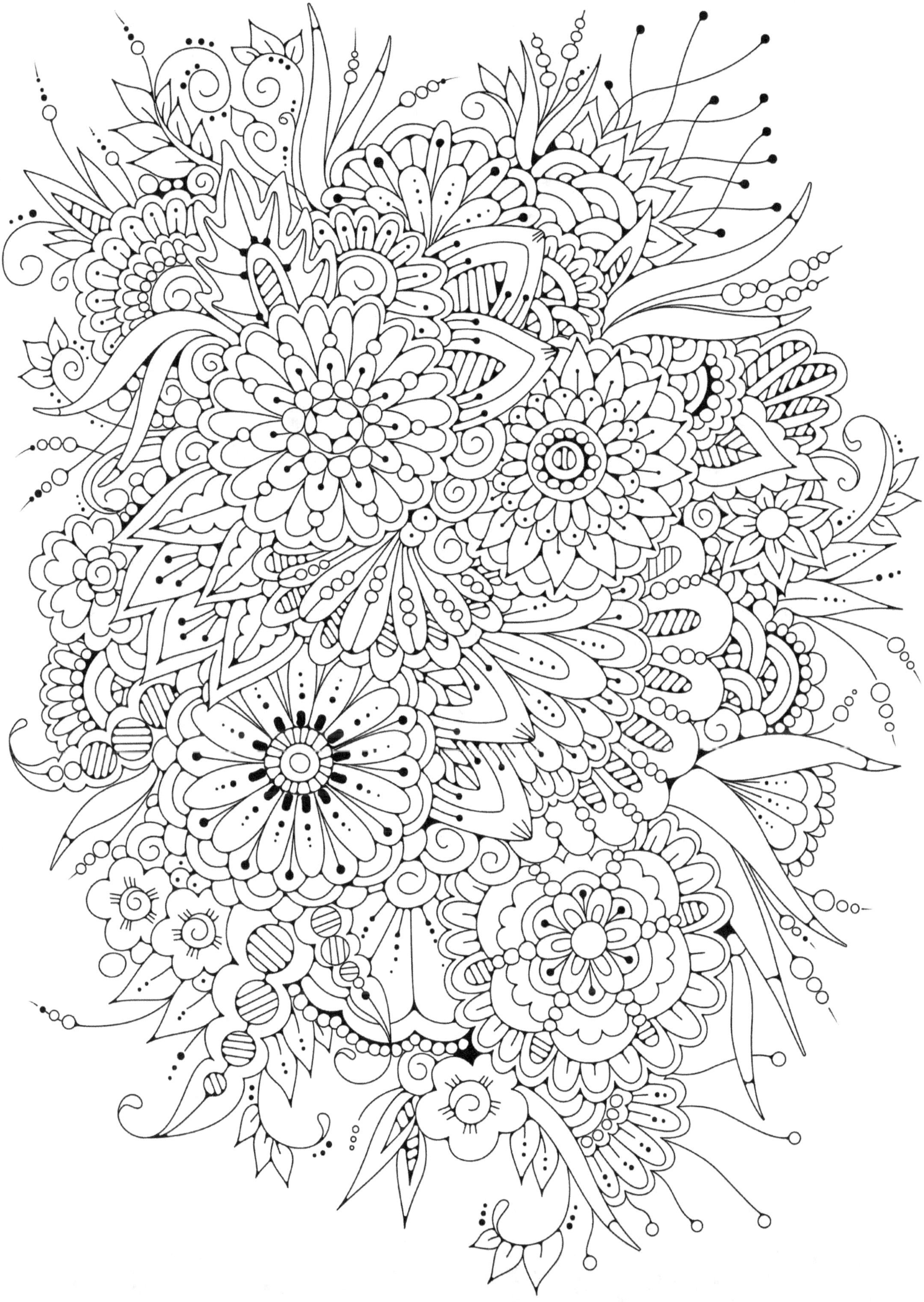

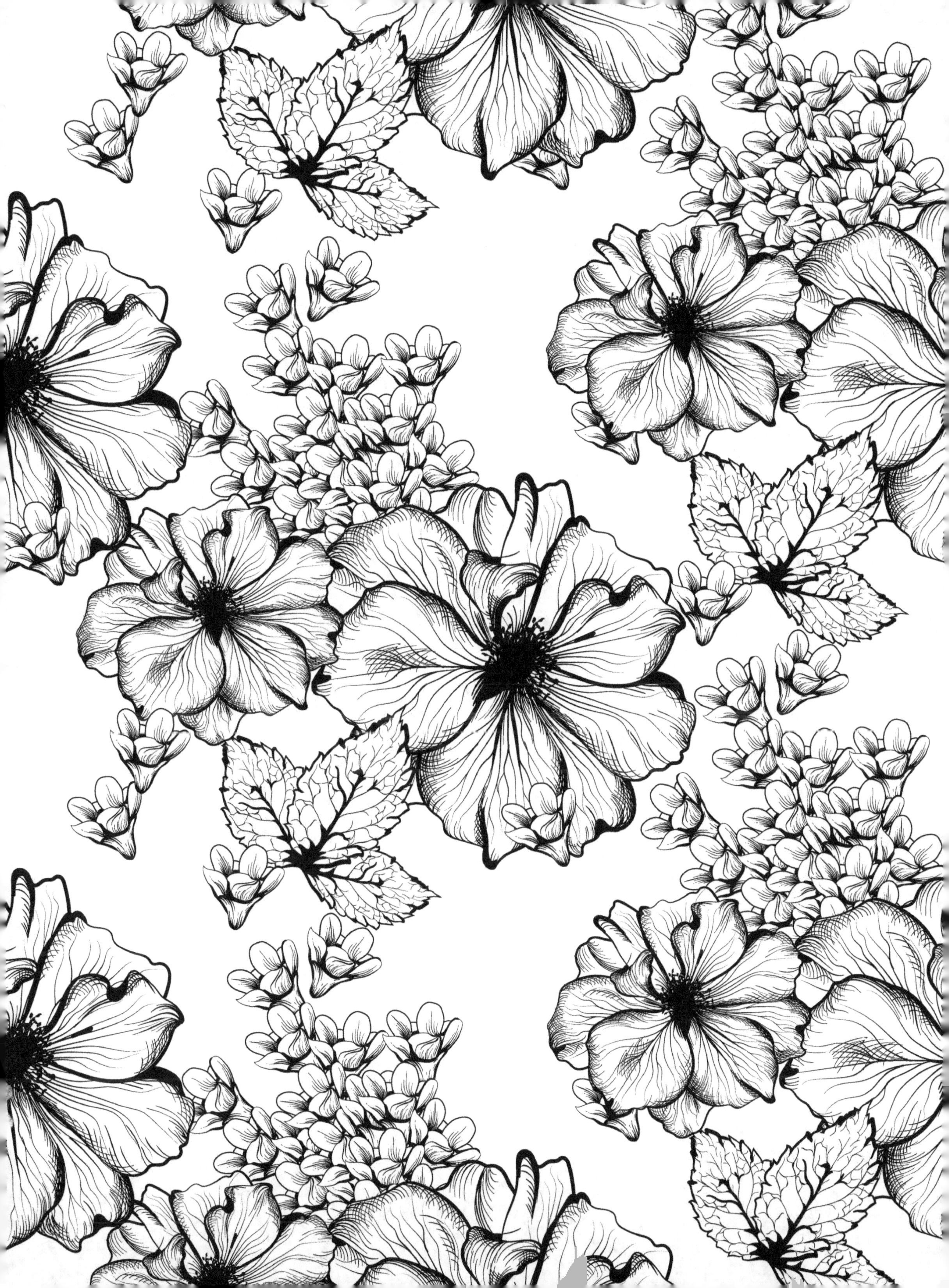

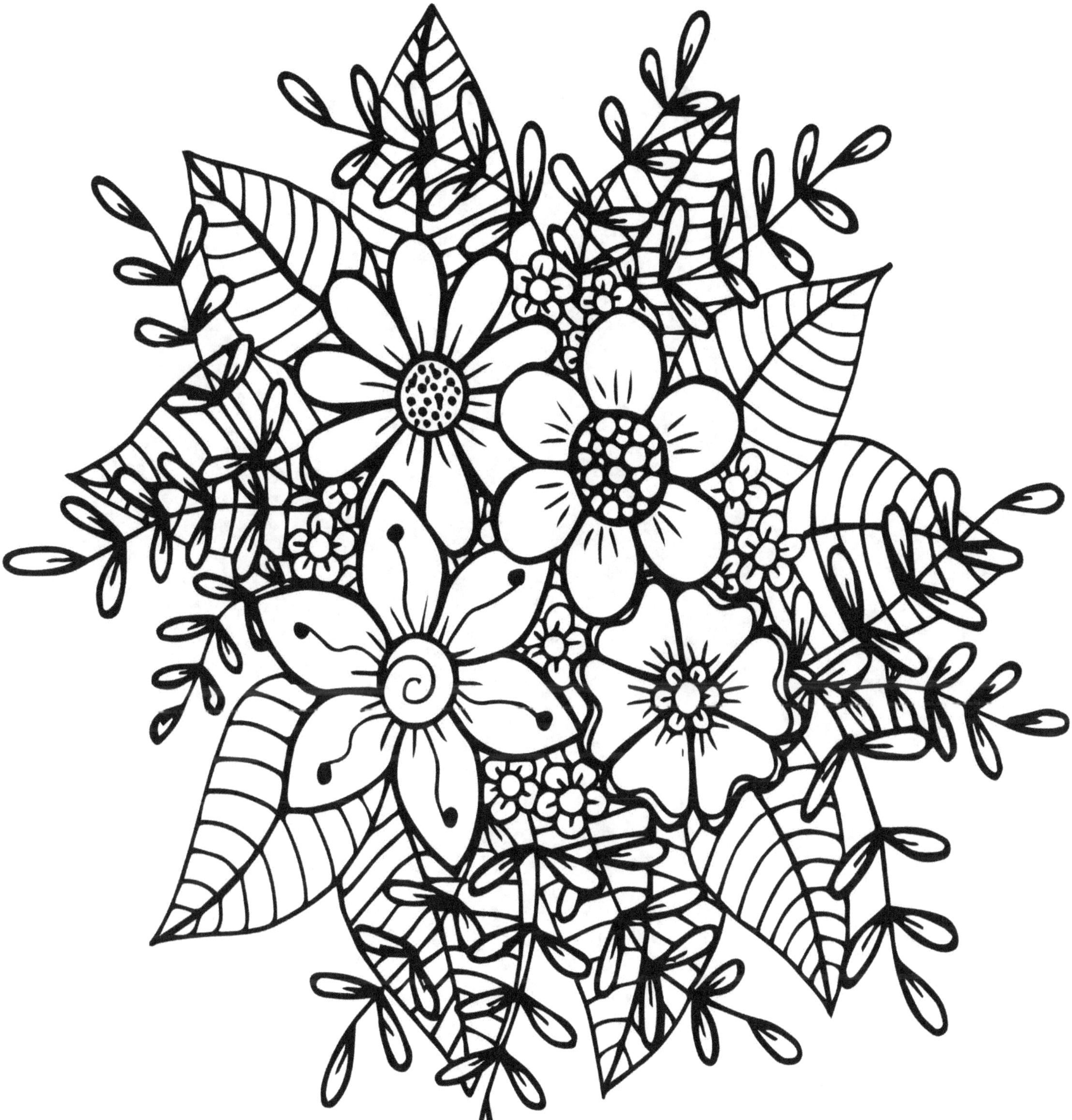

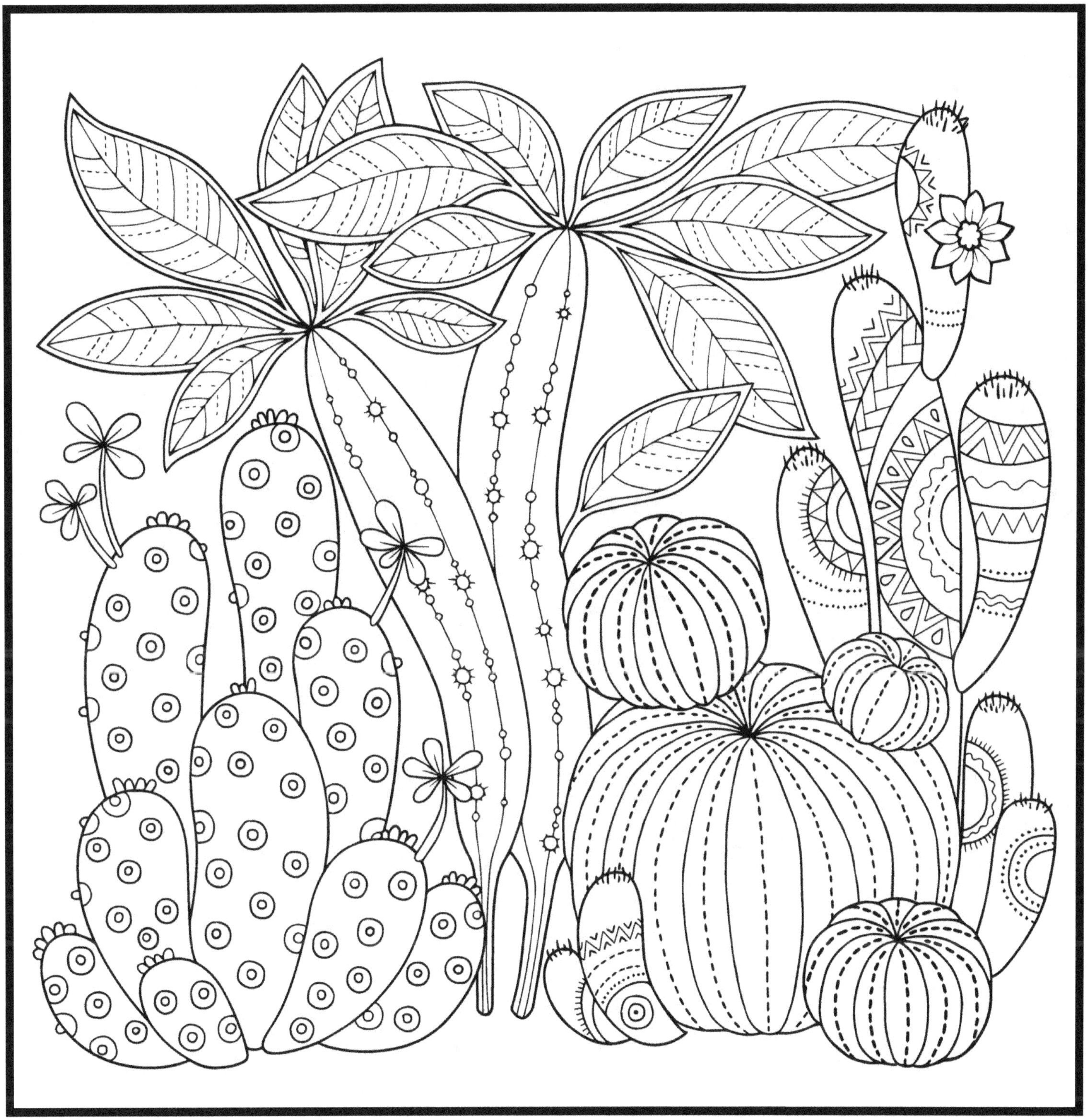

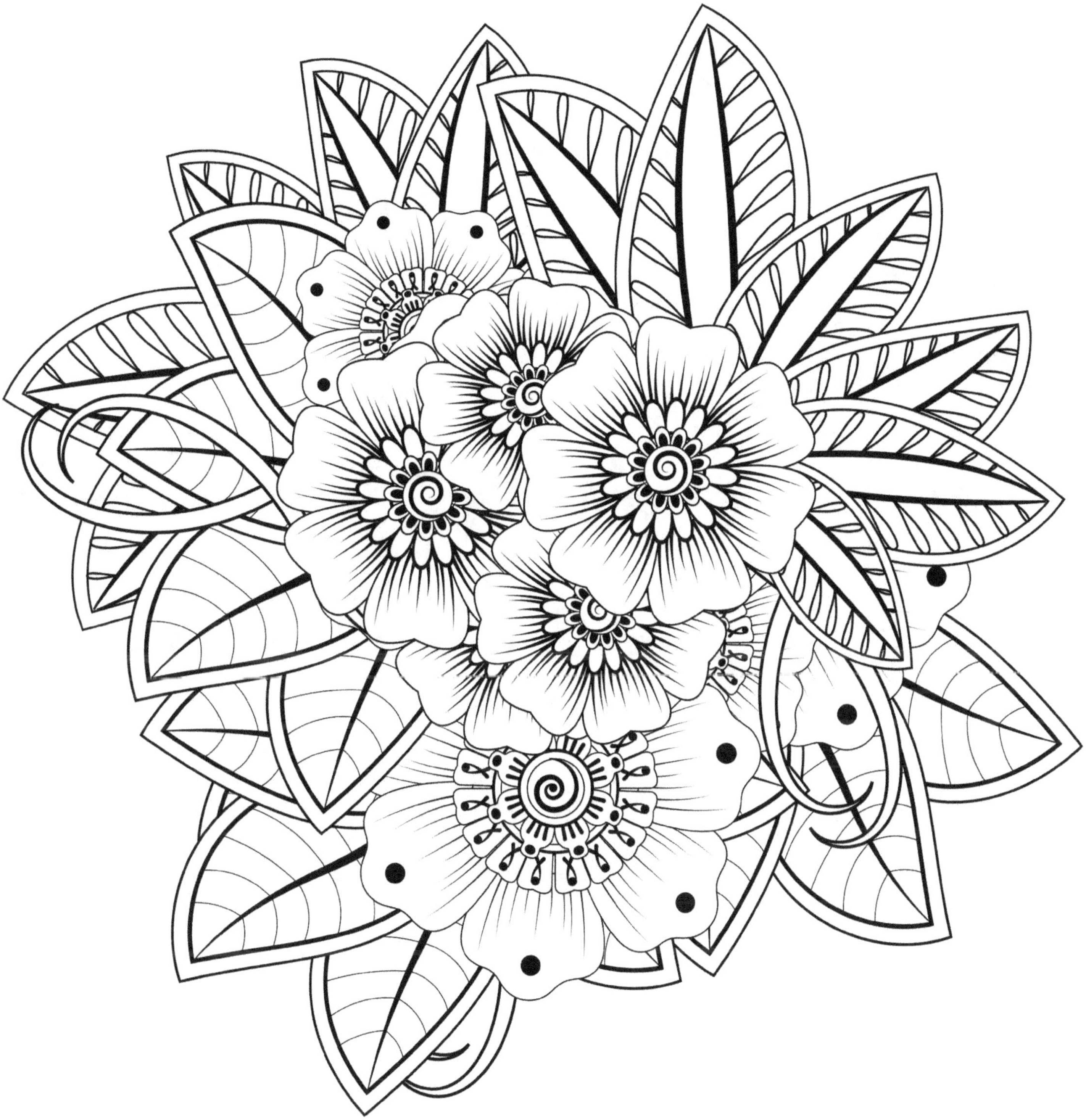

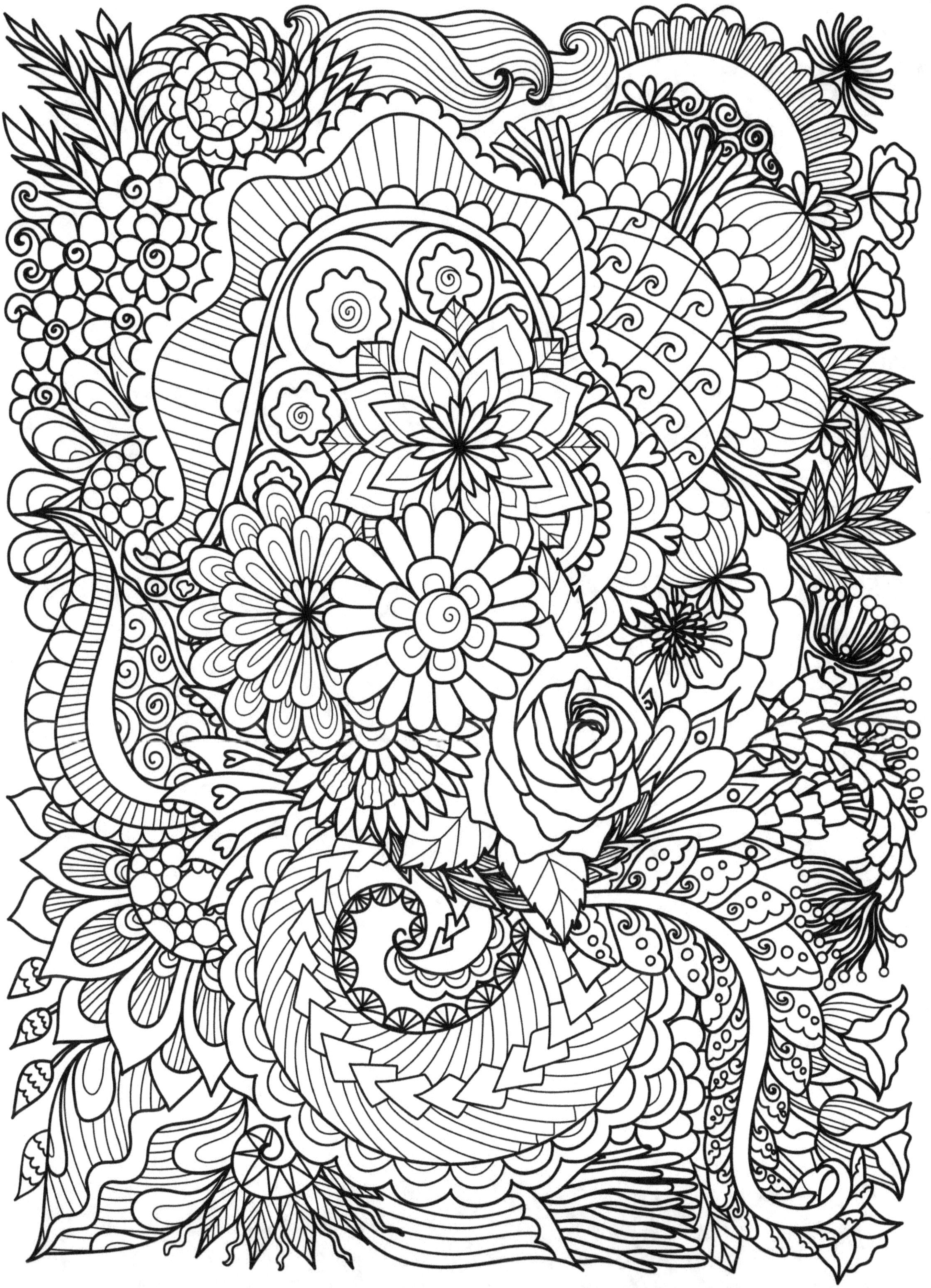

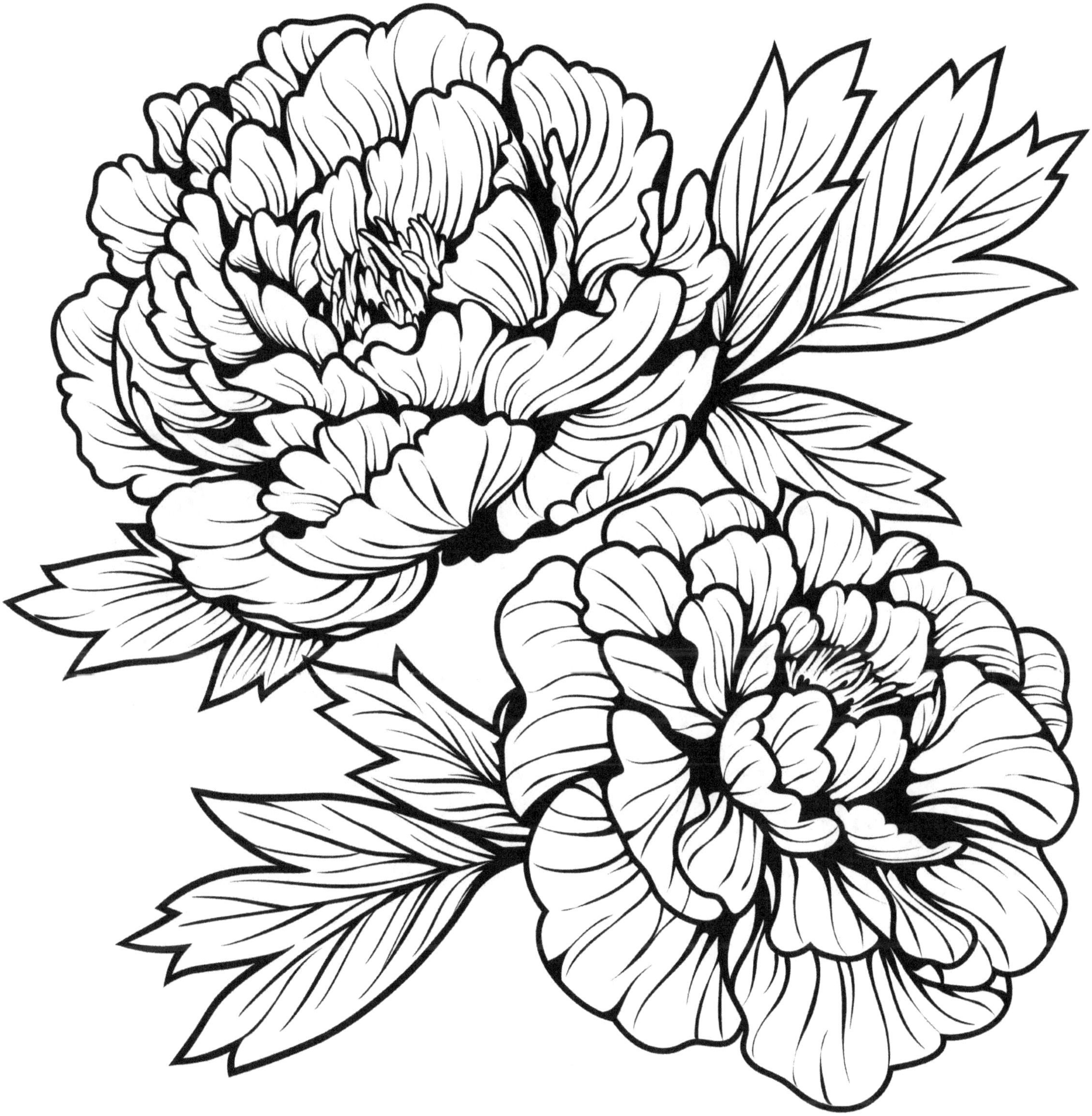

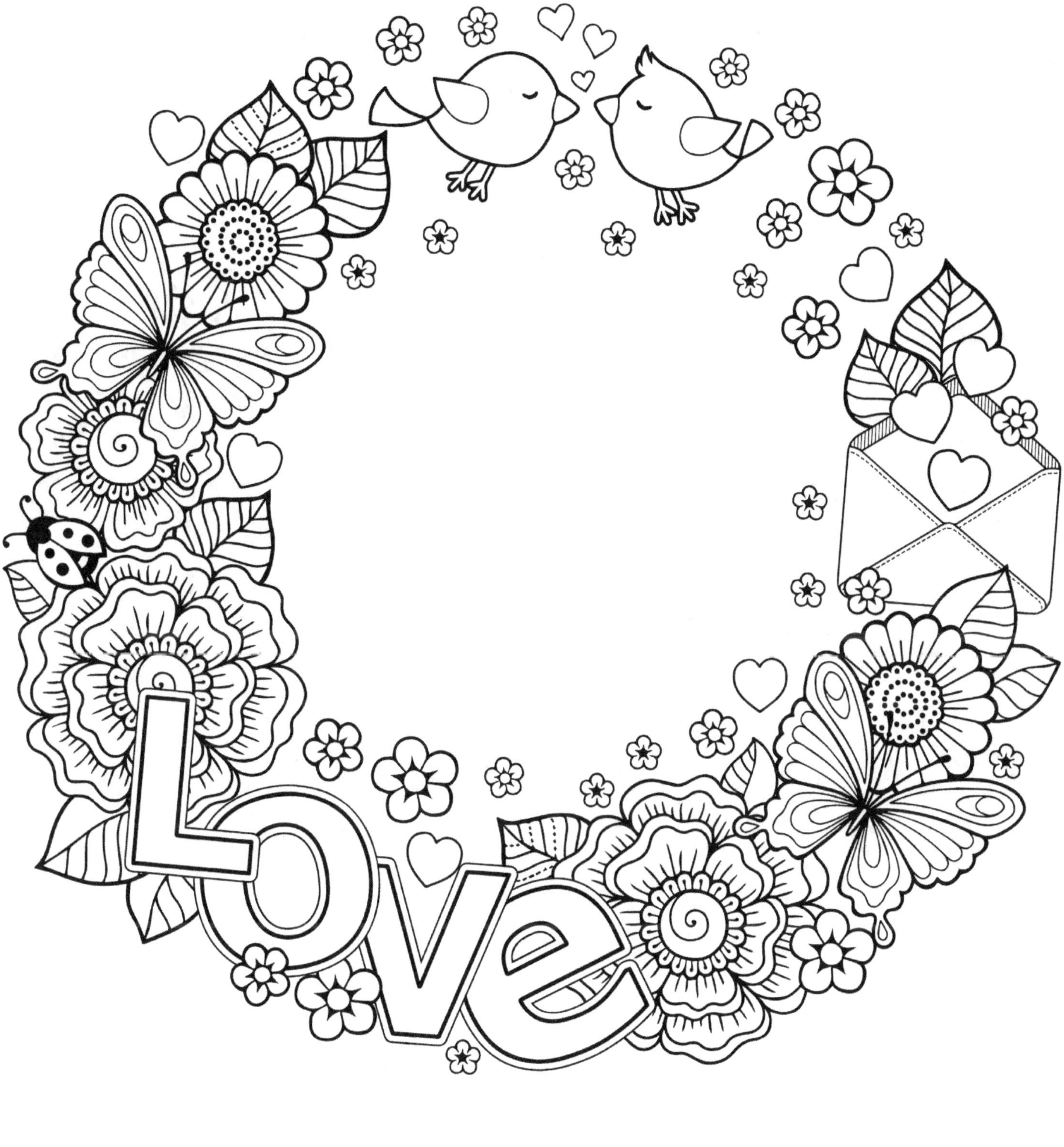
Love

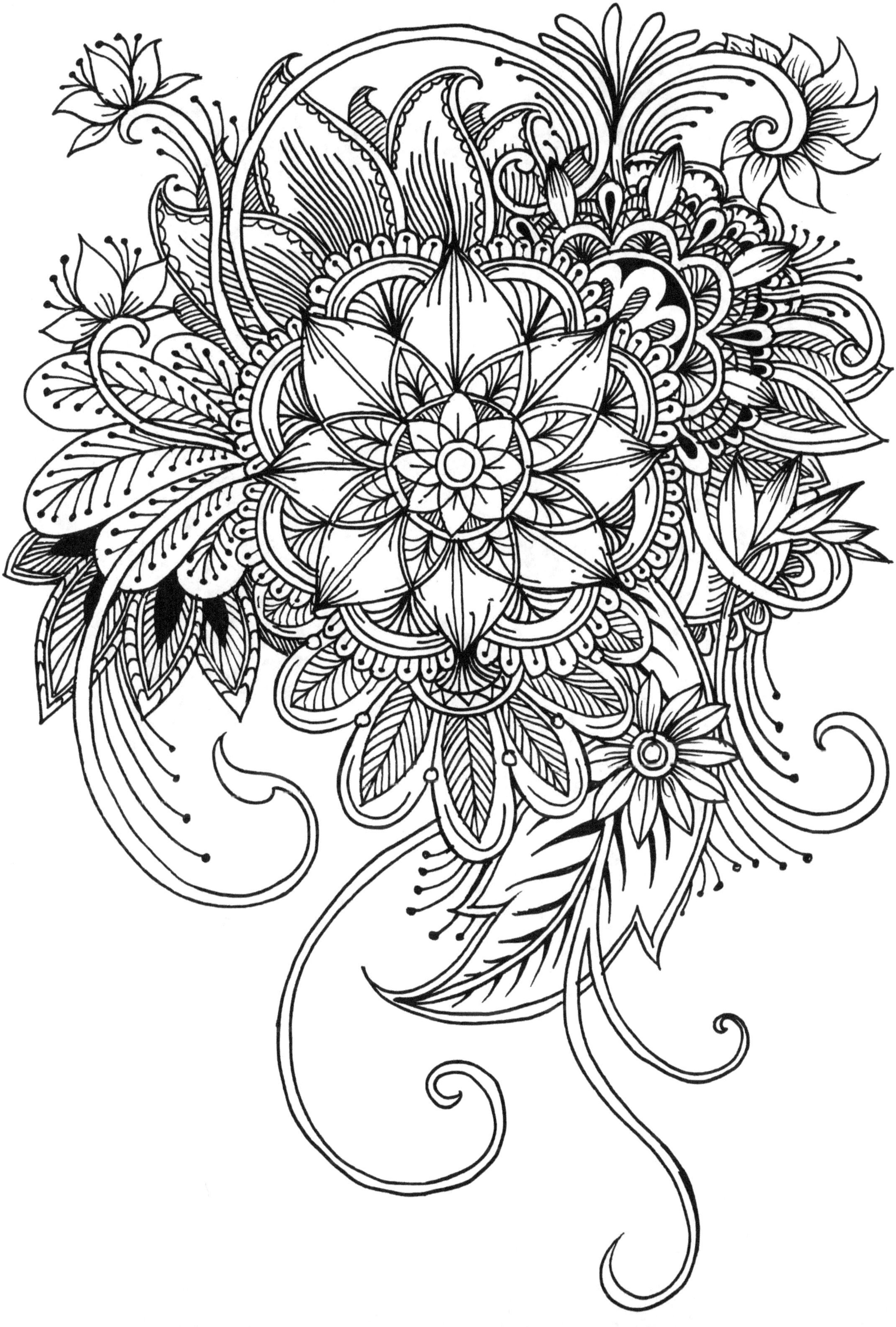

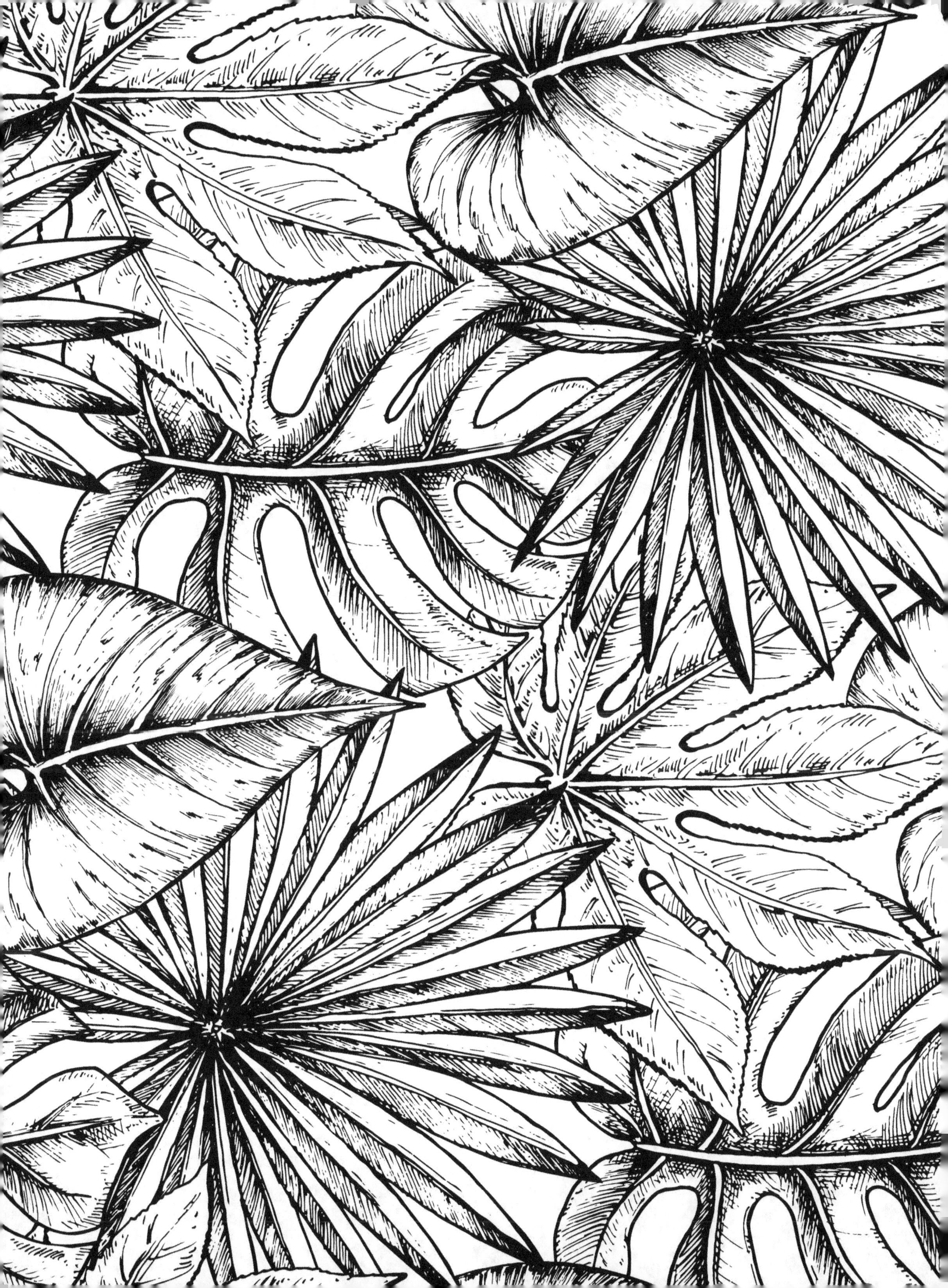

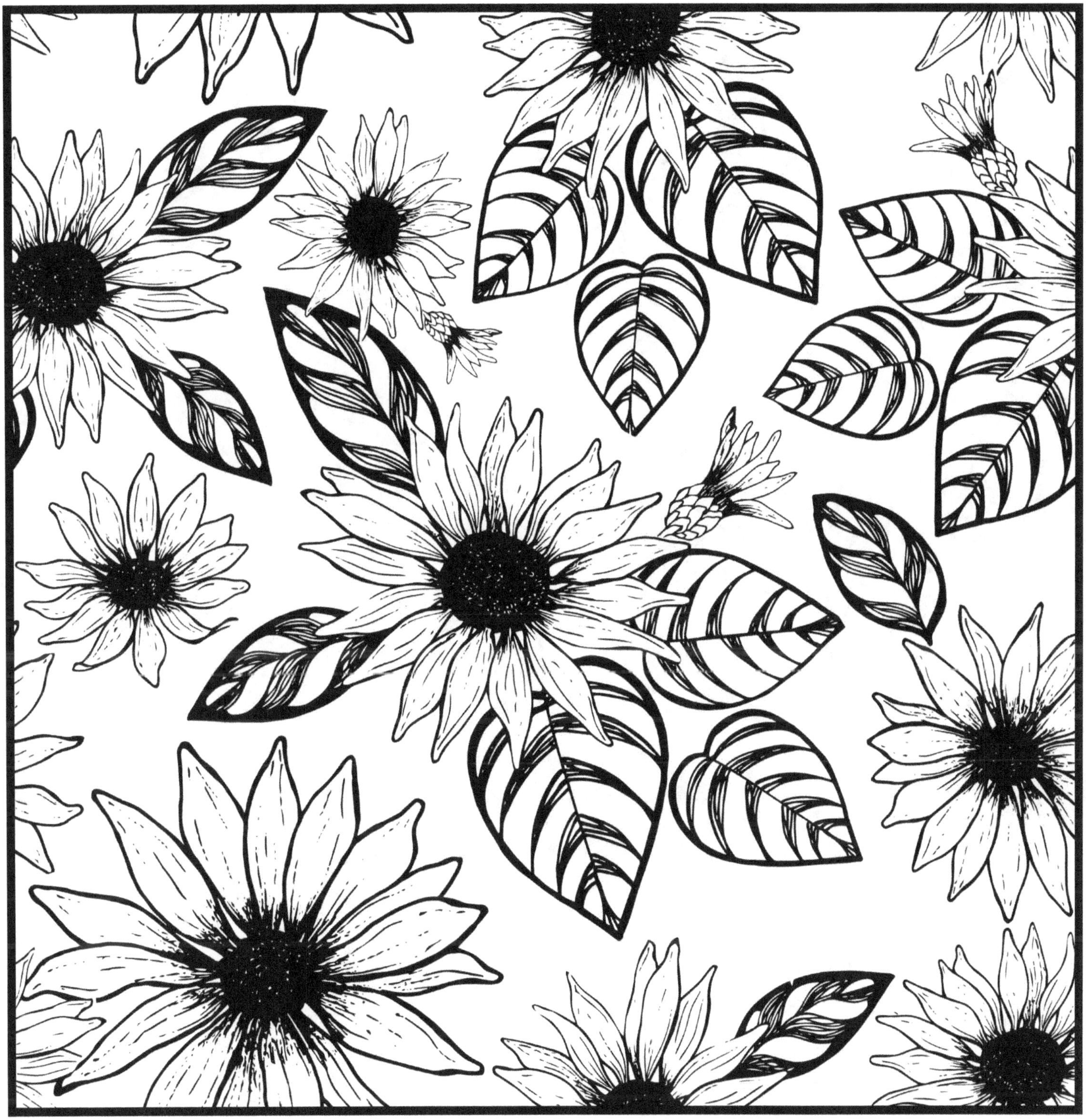

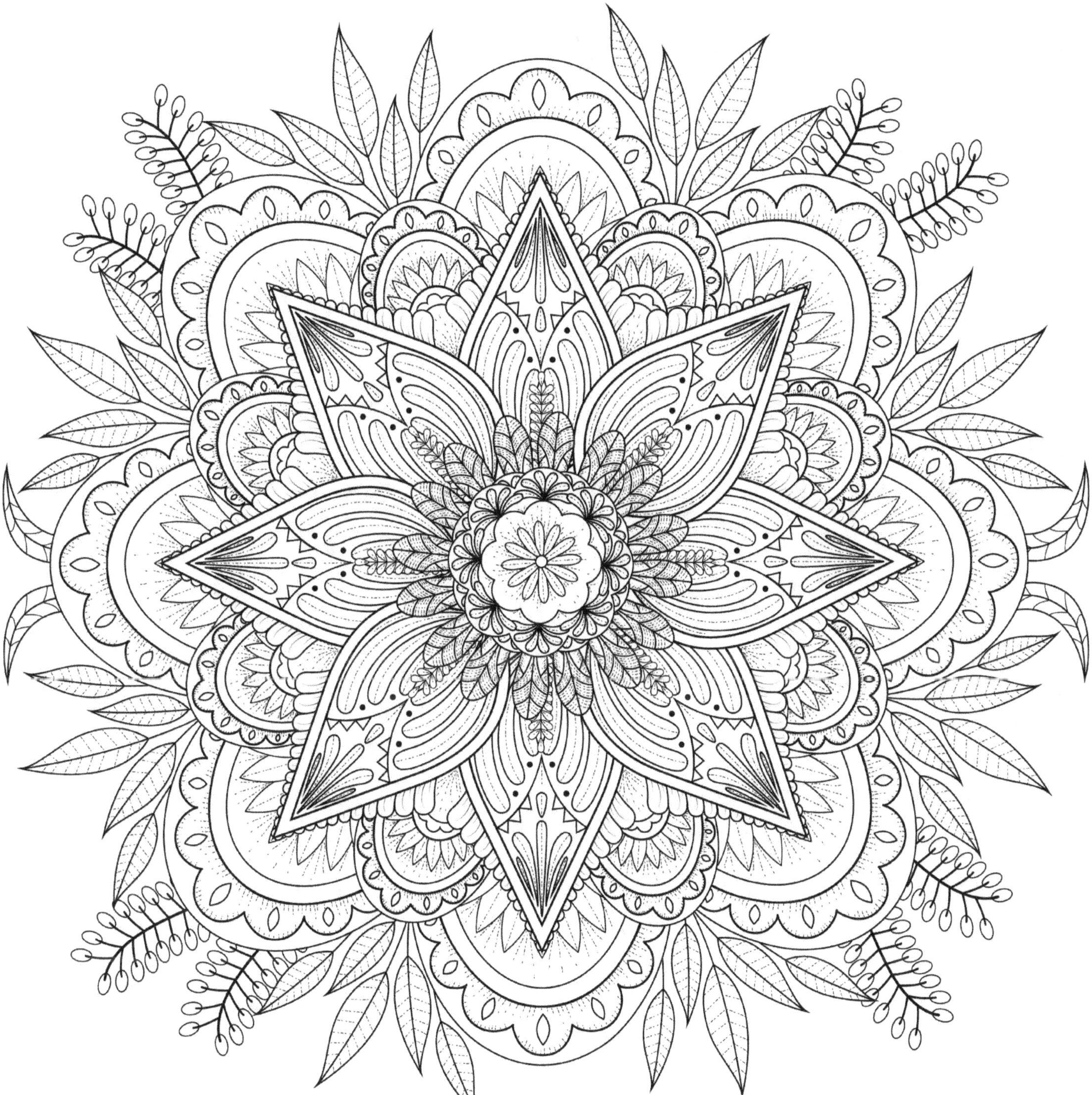

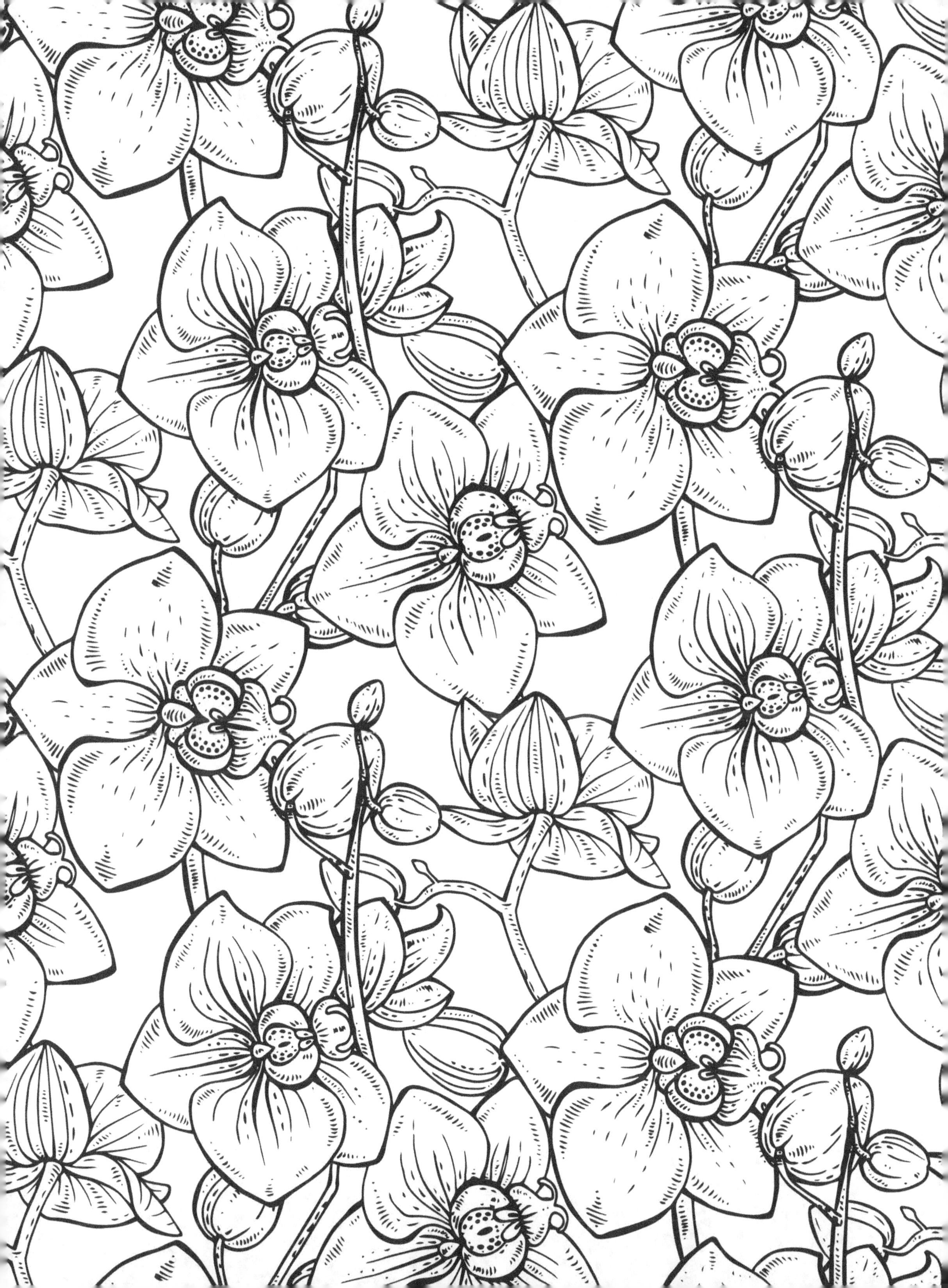

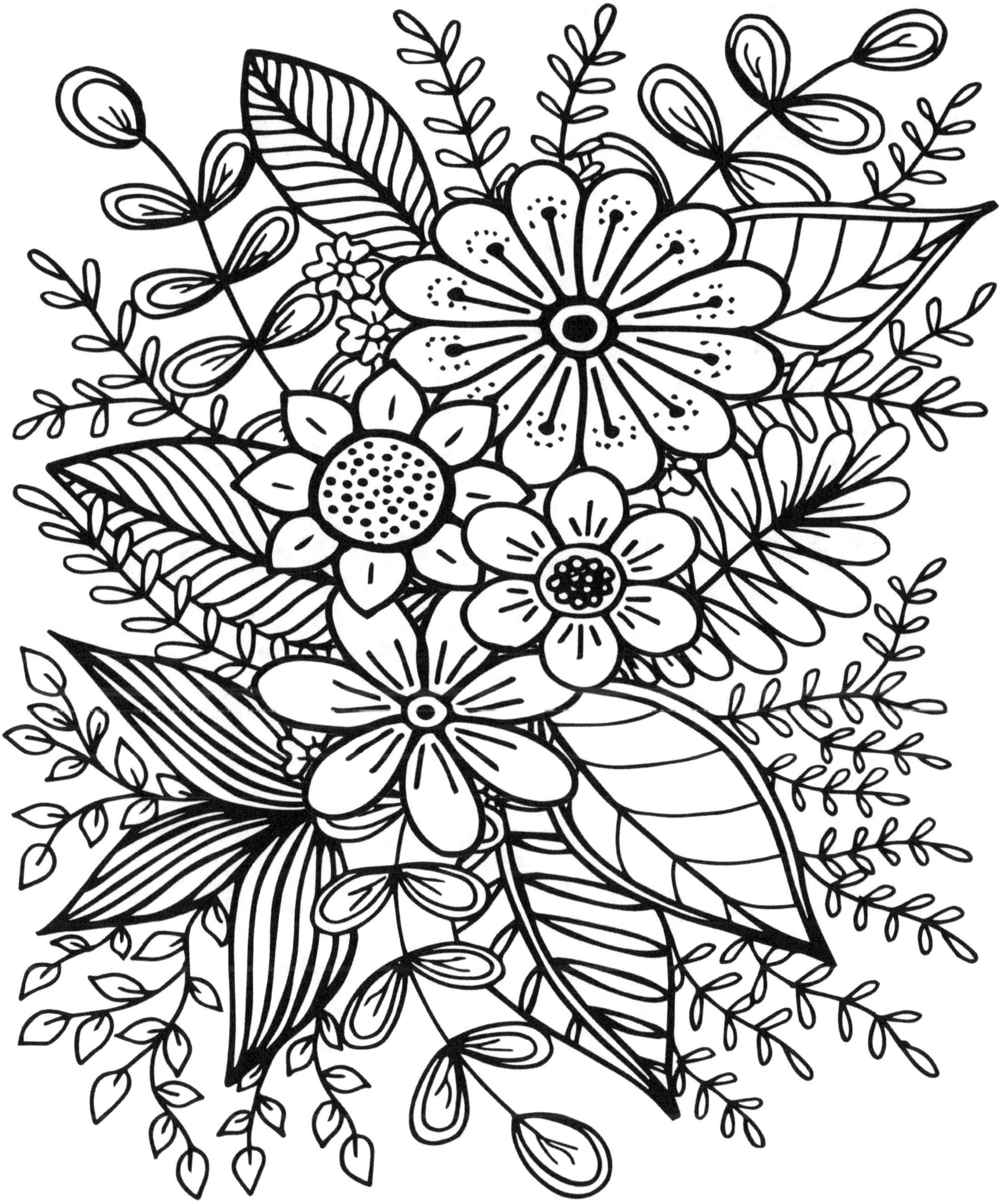

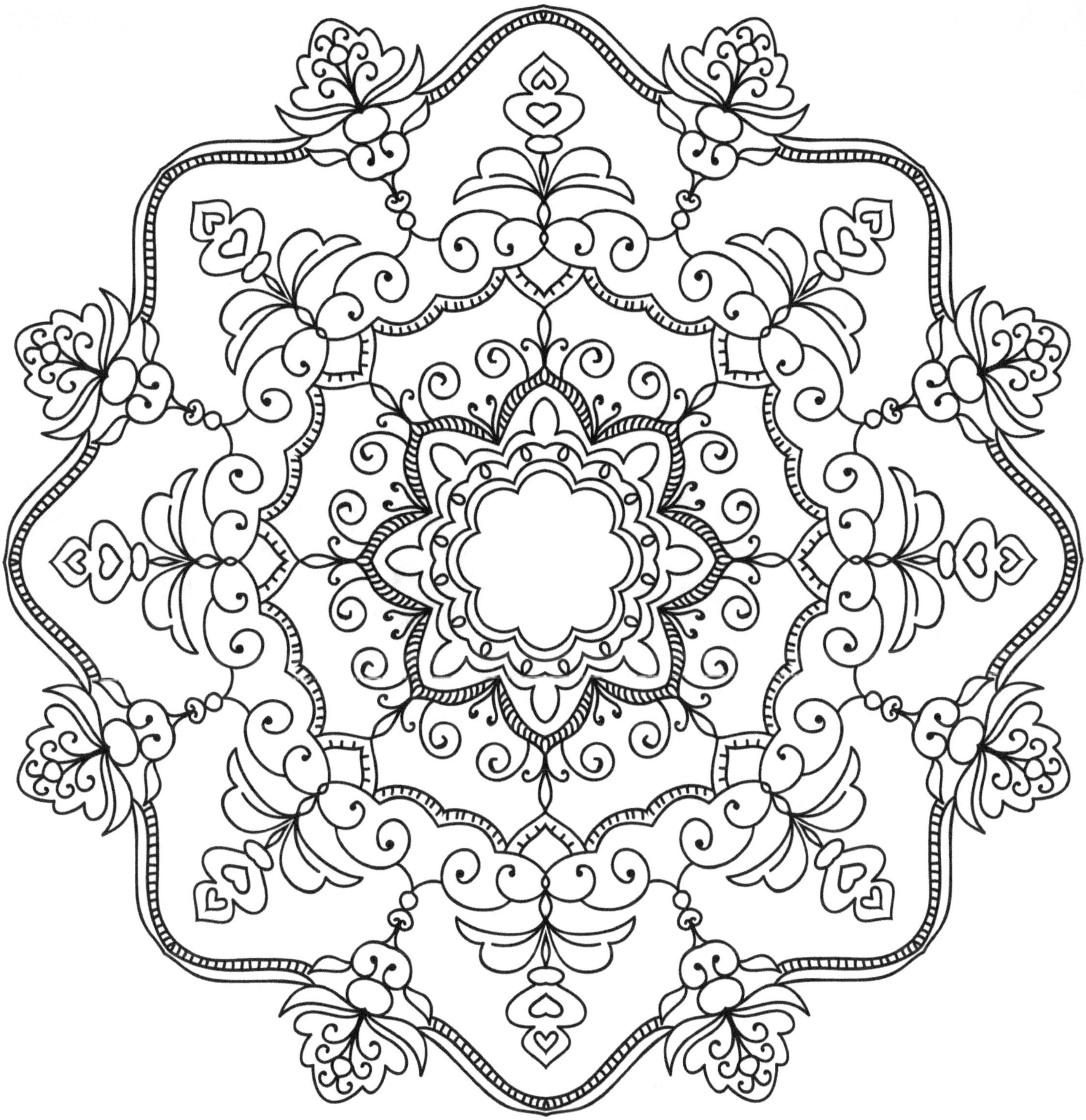

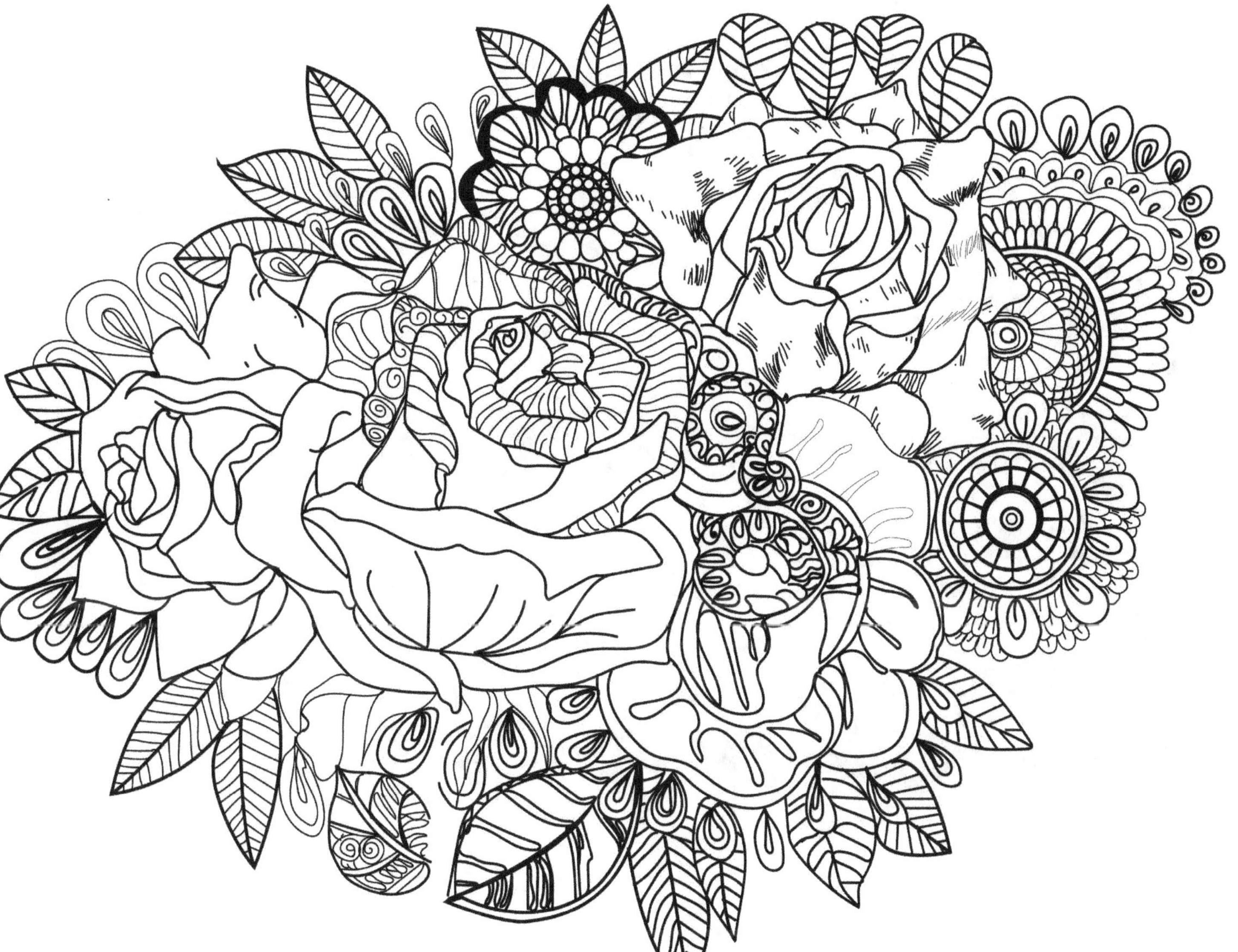

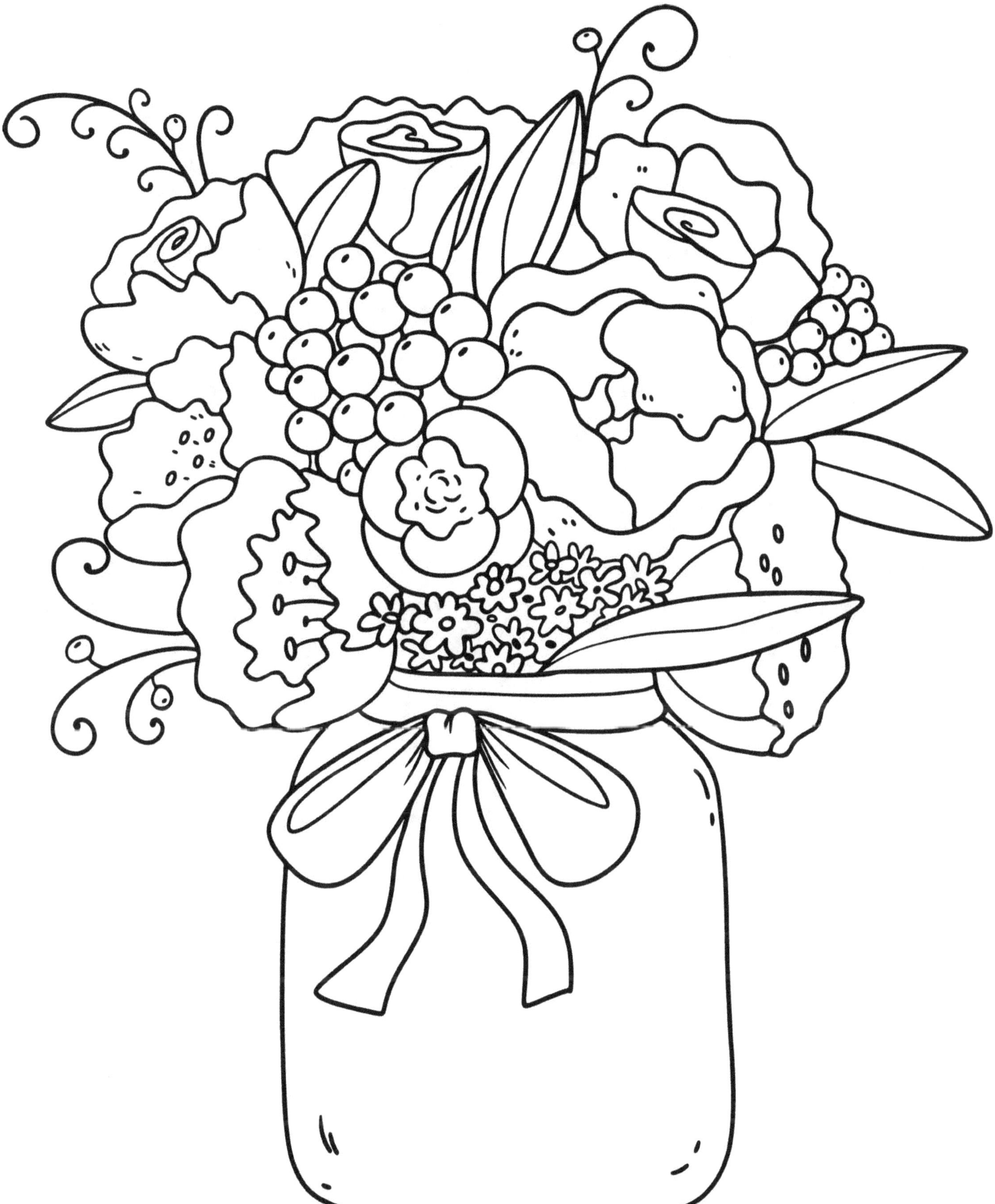

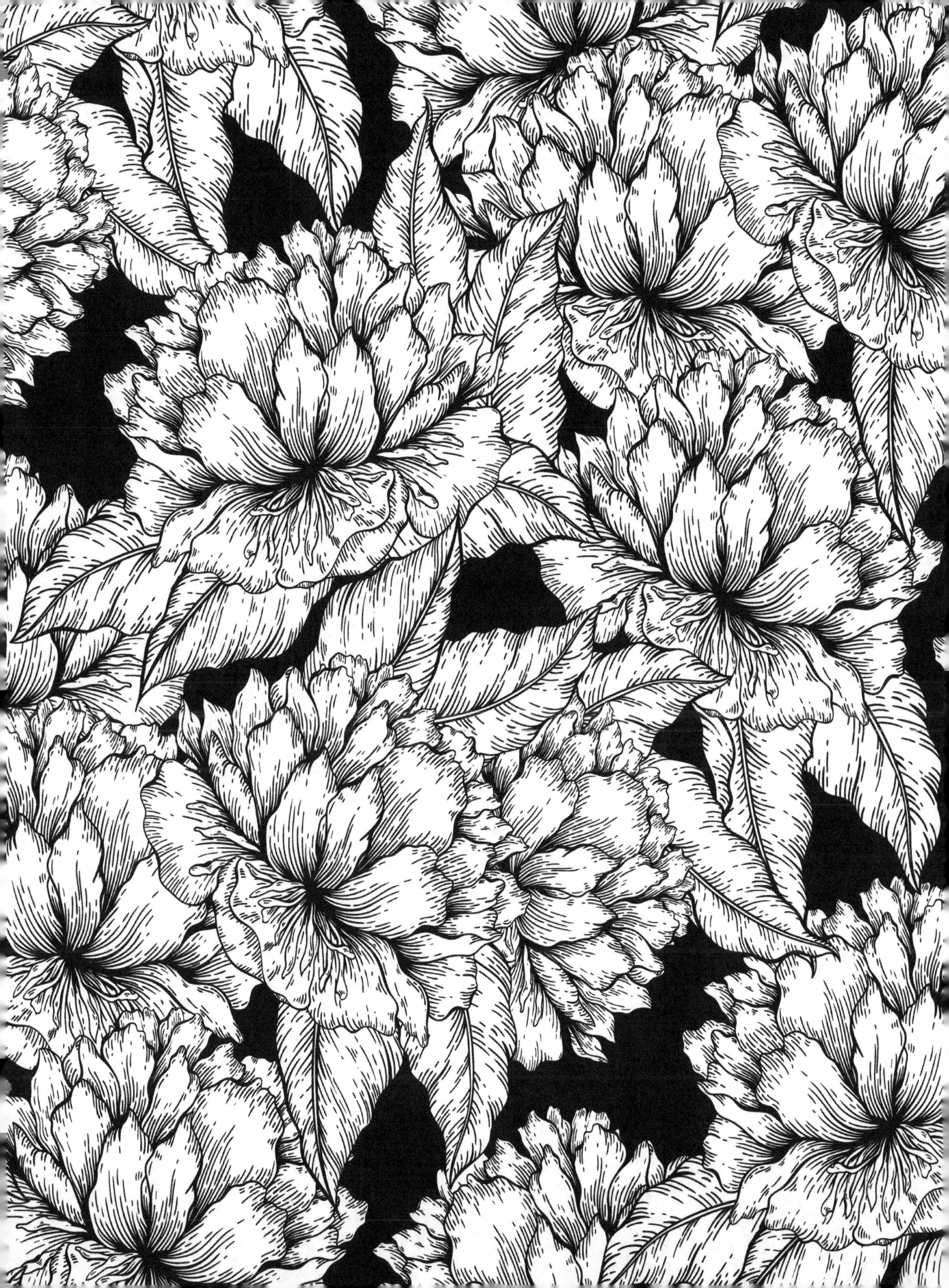

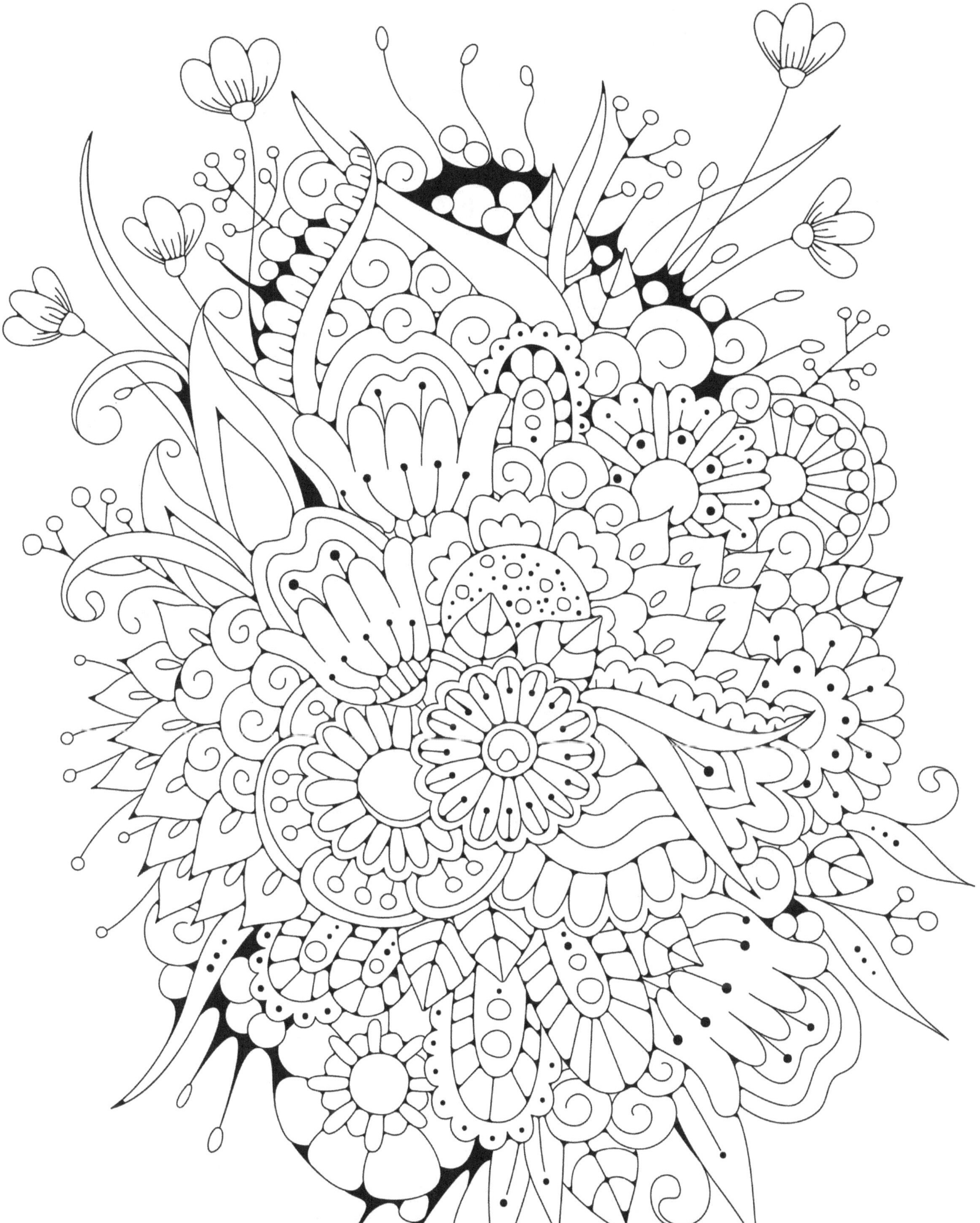

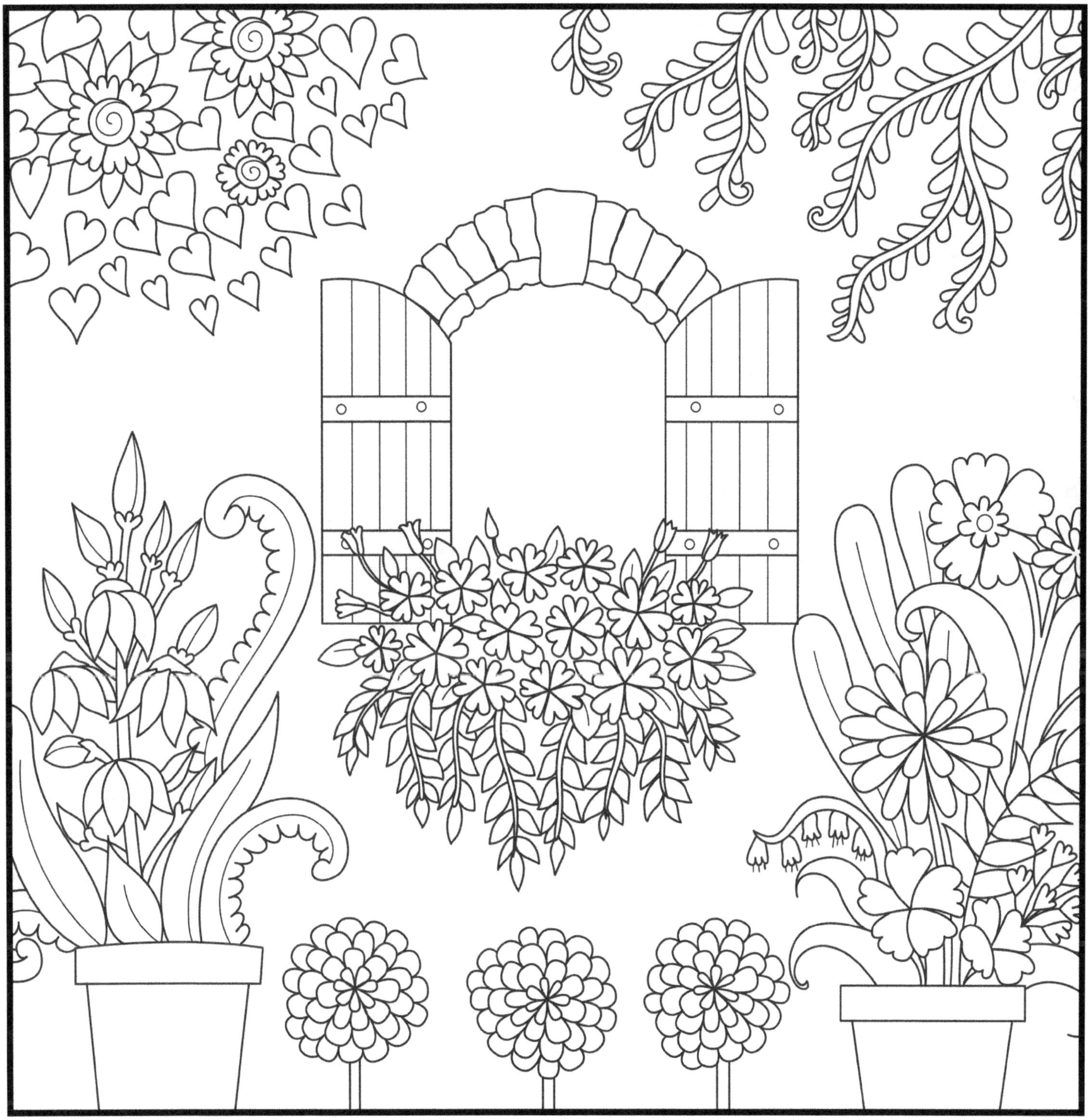

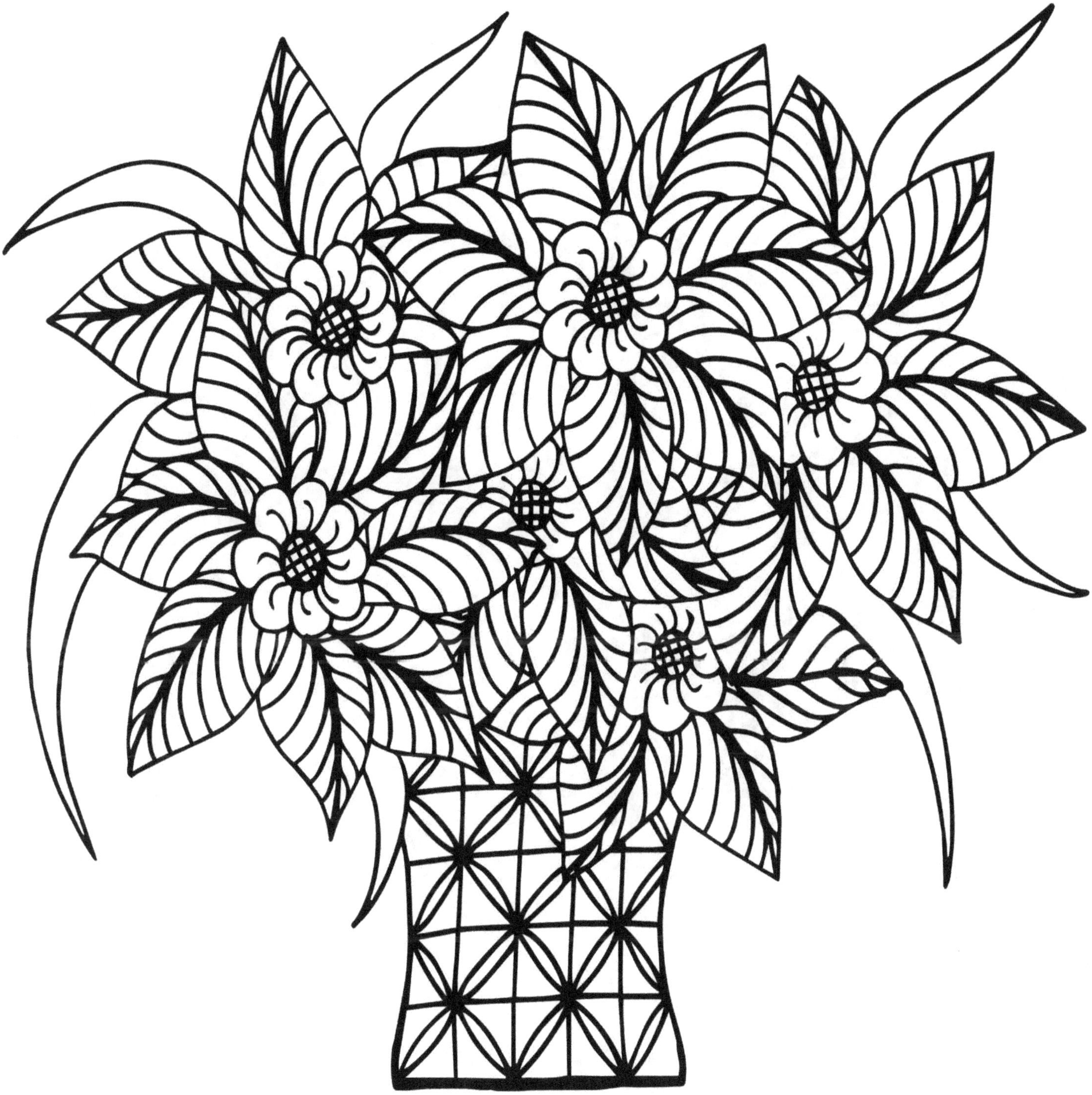

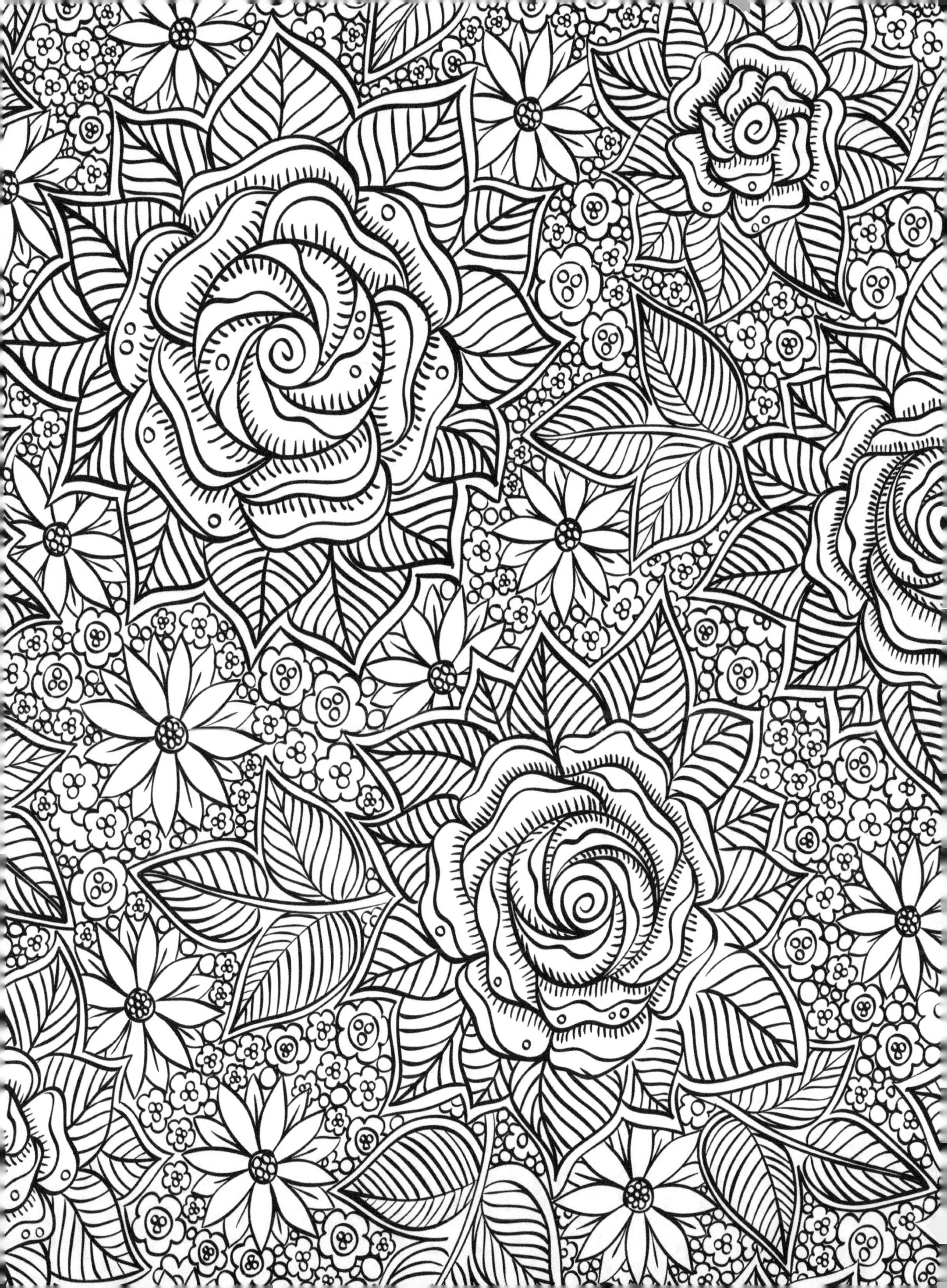

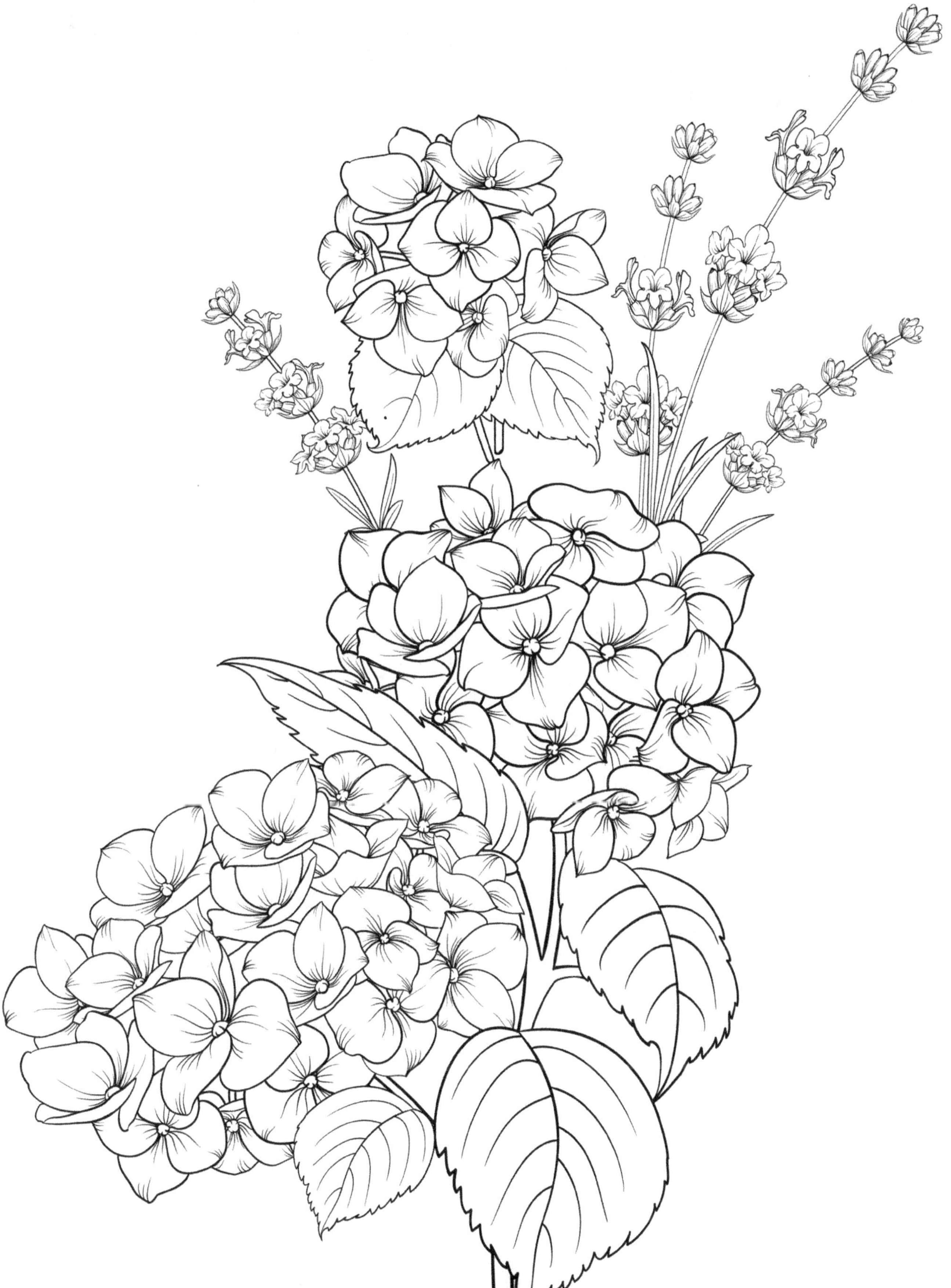

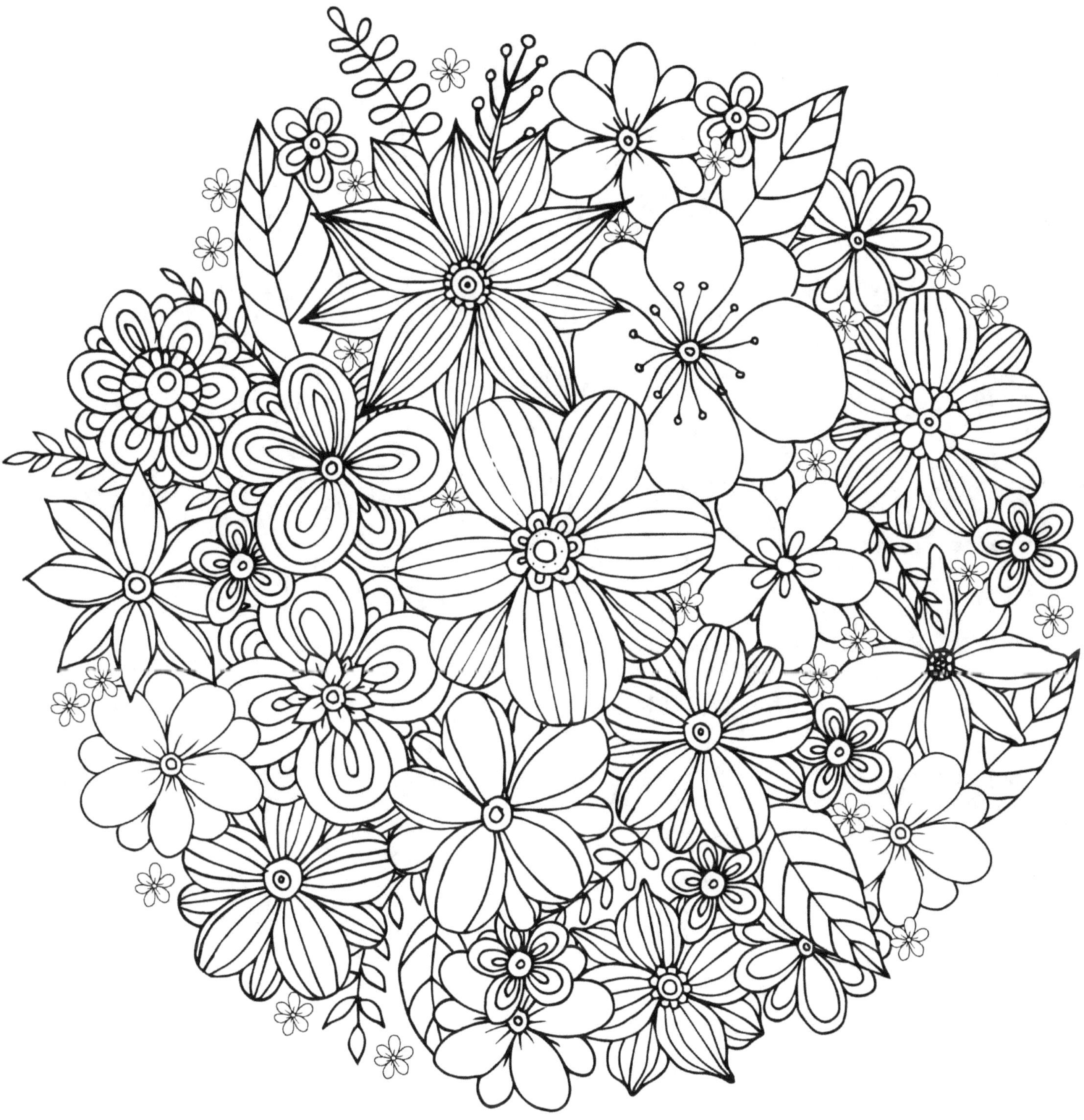

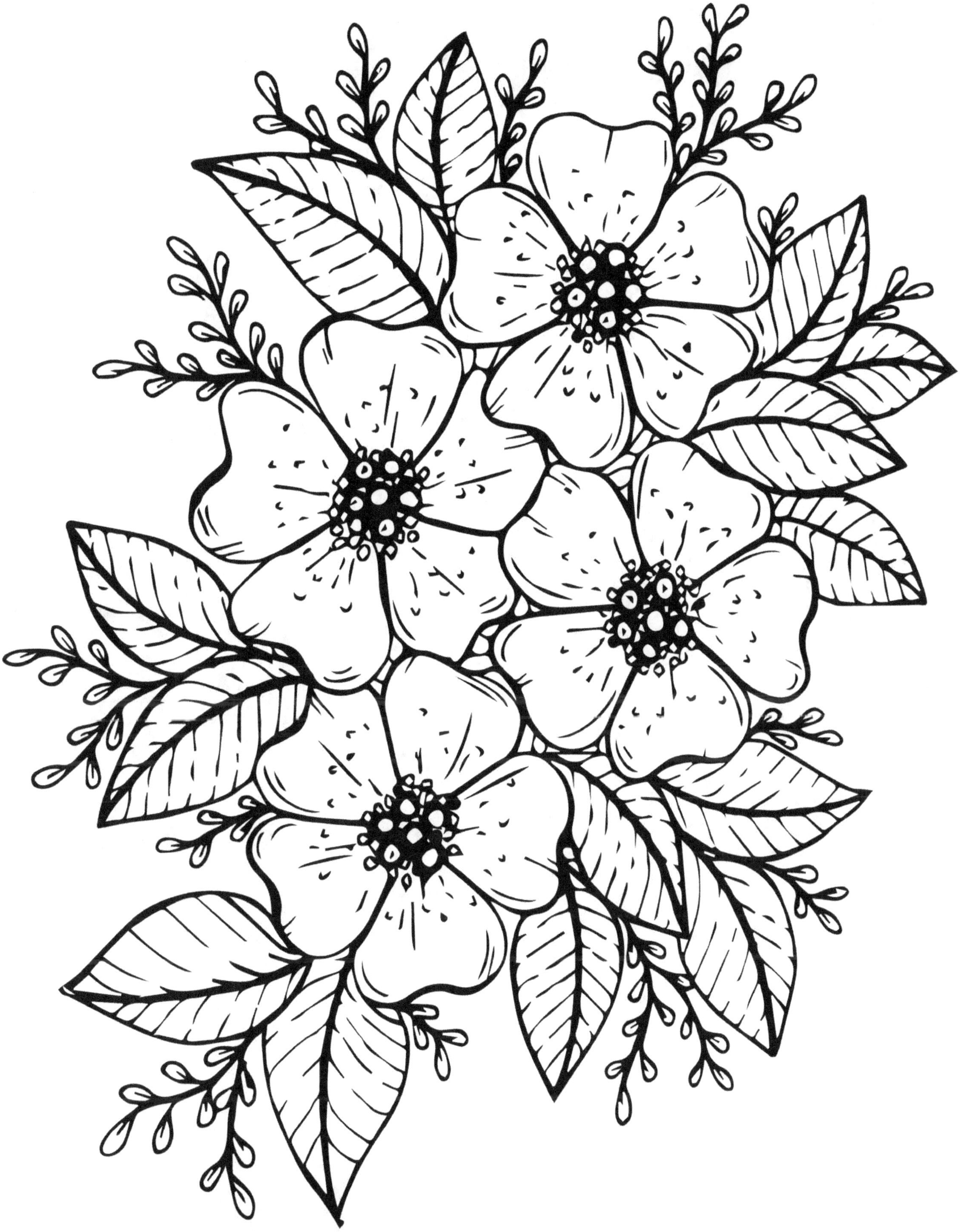

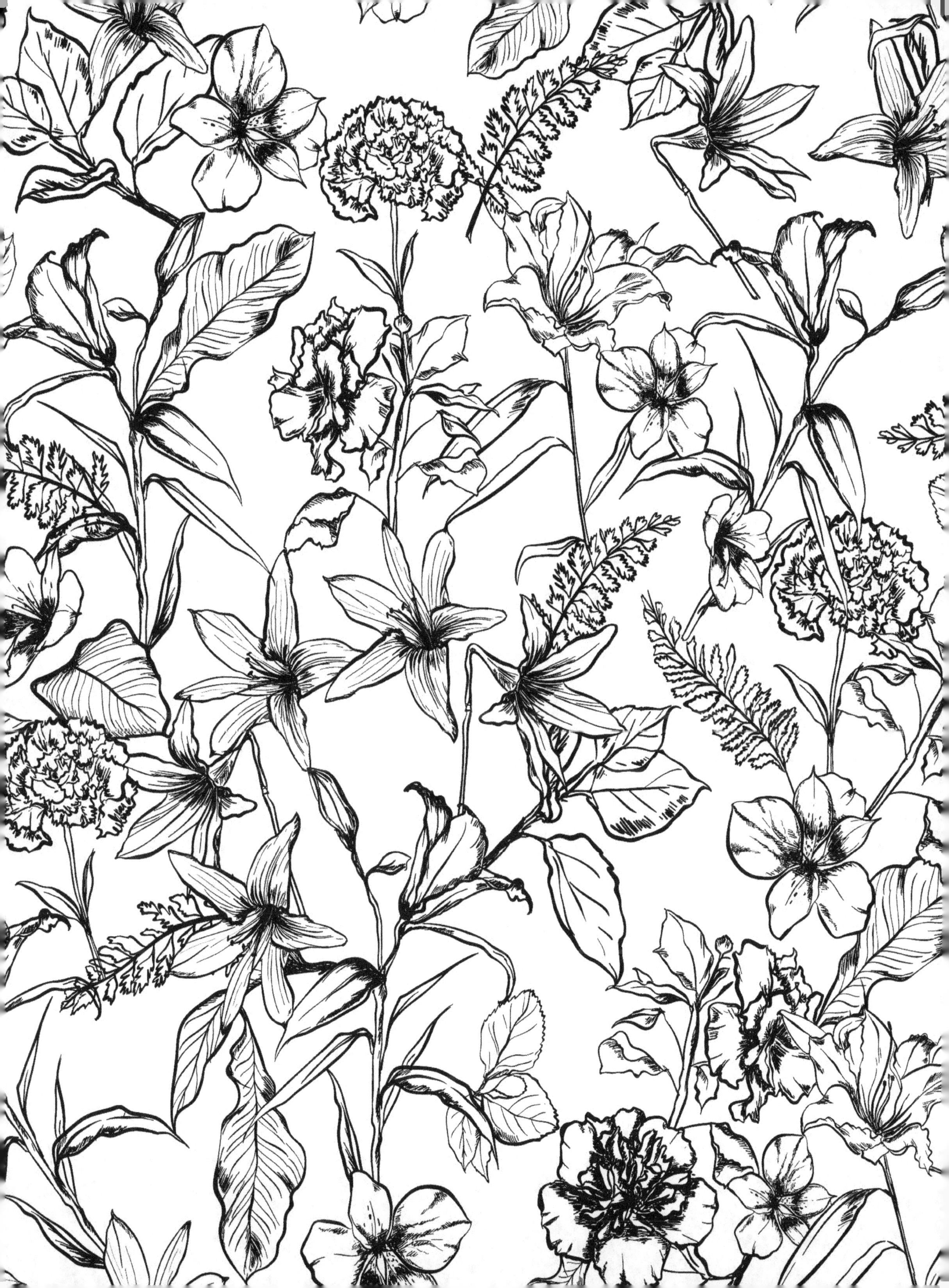

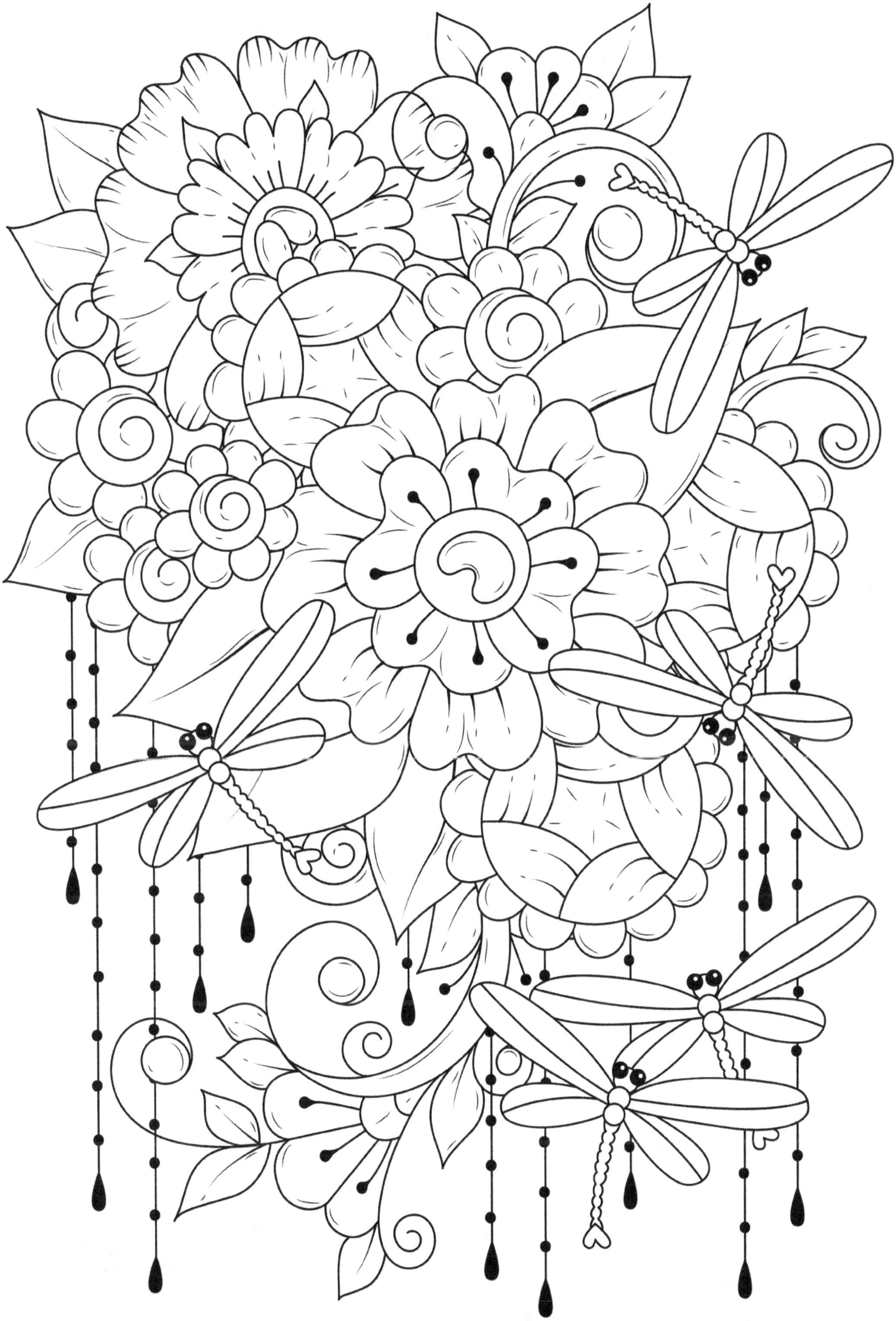

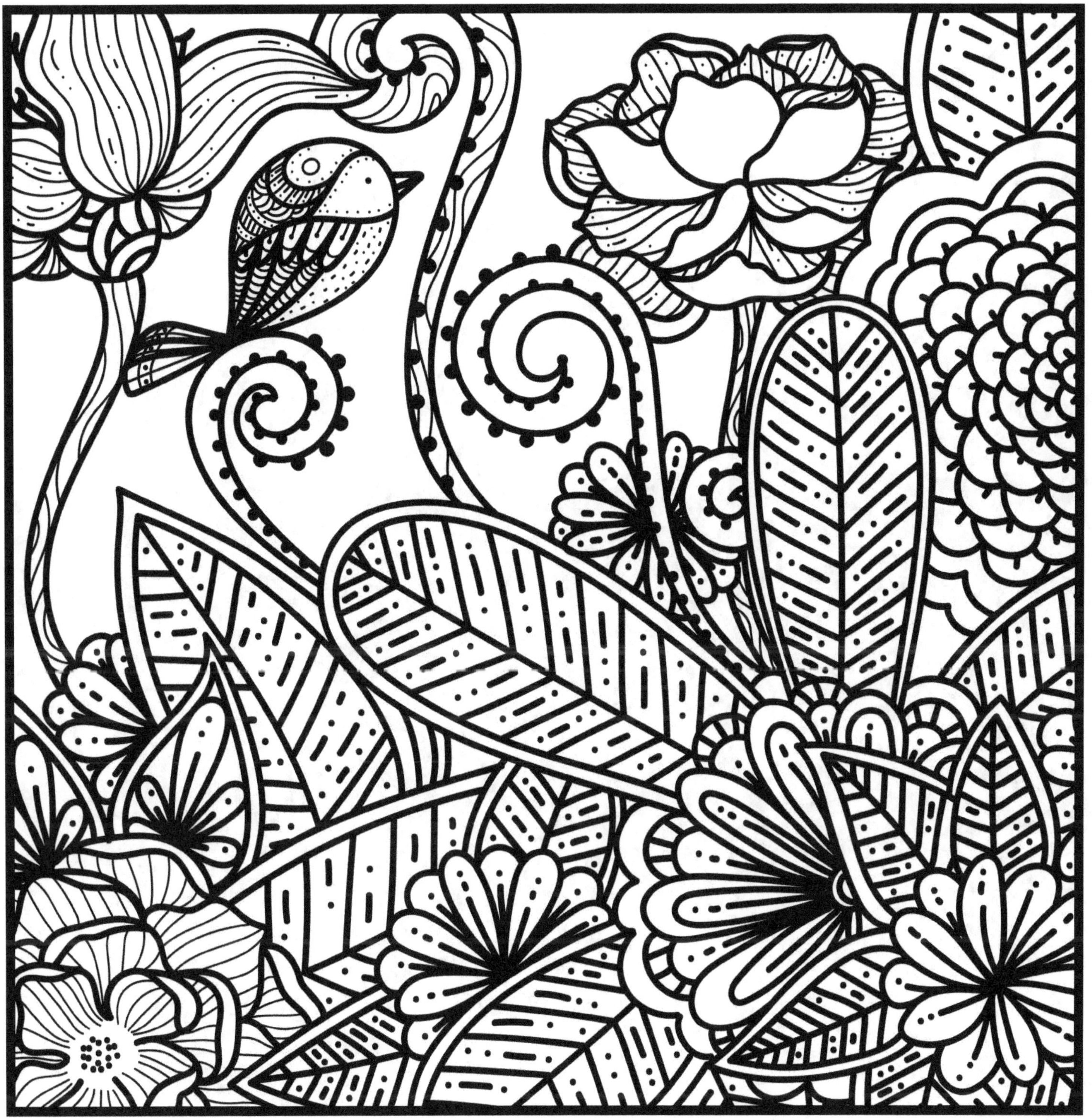

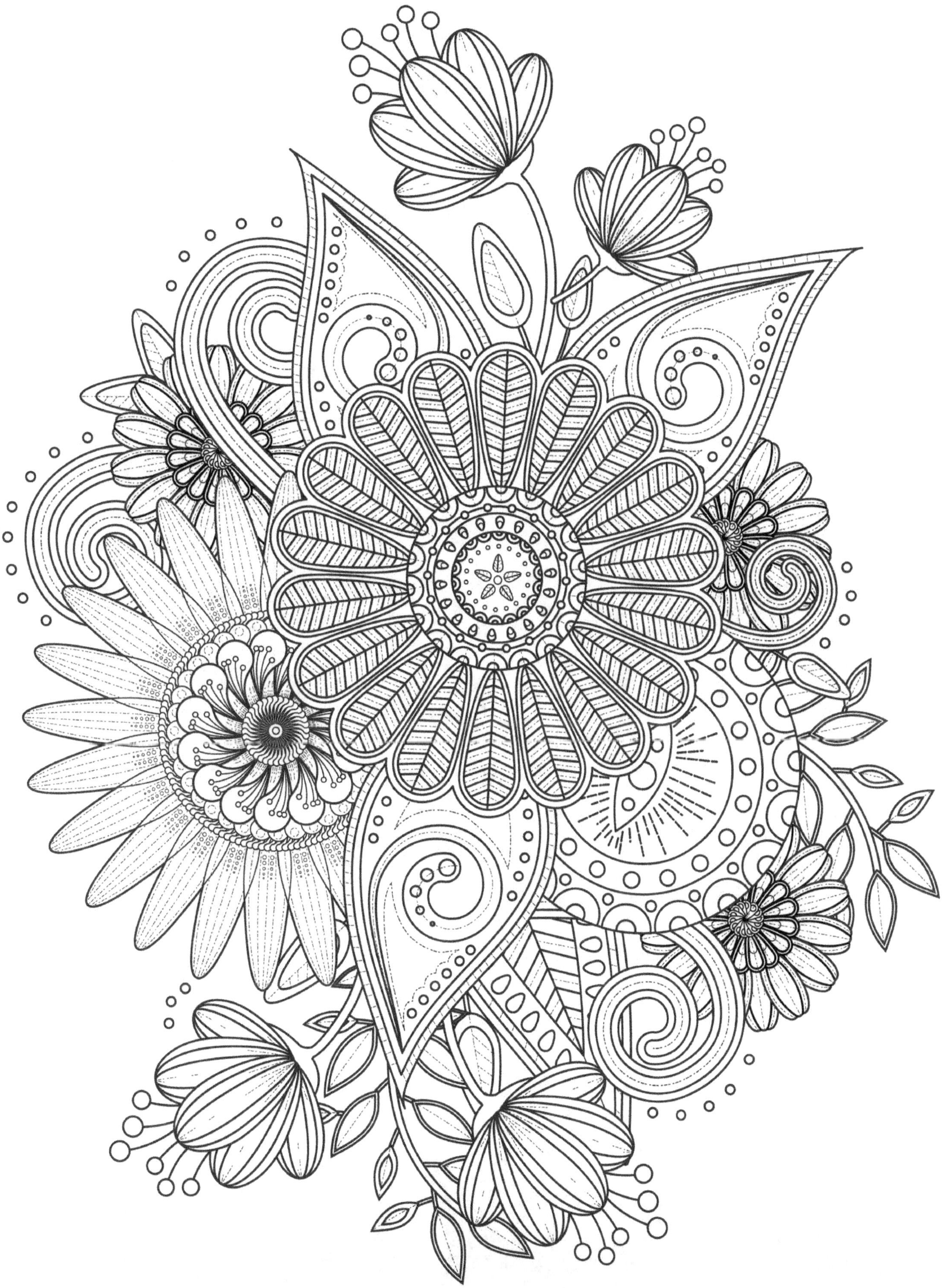

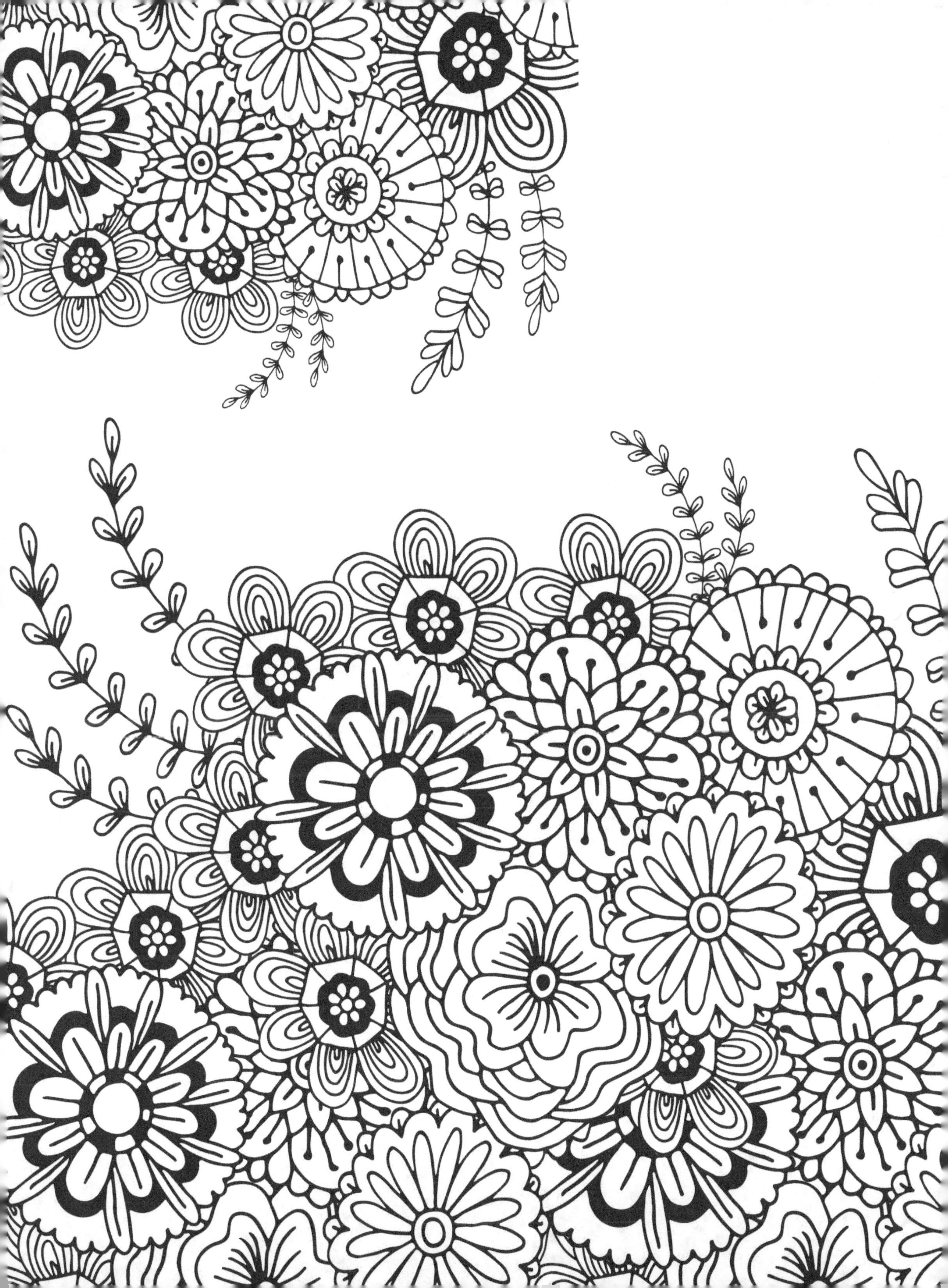

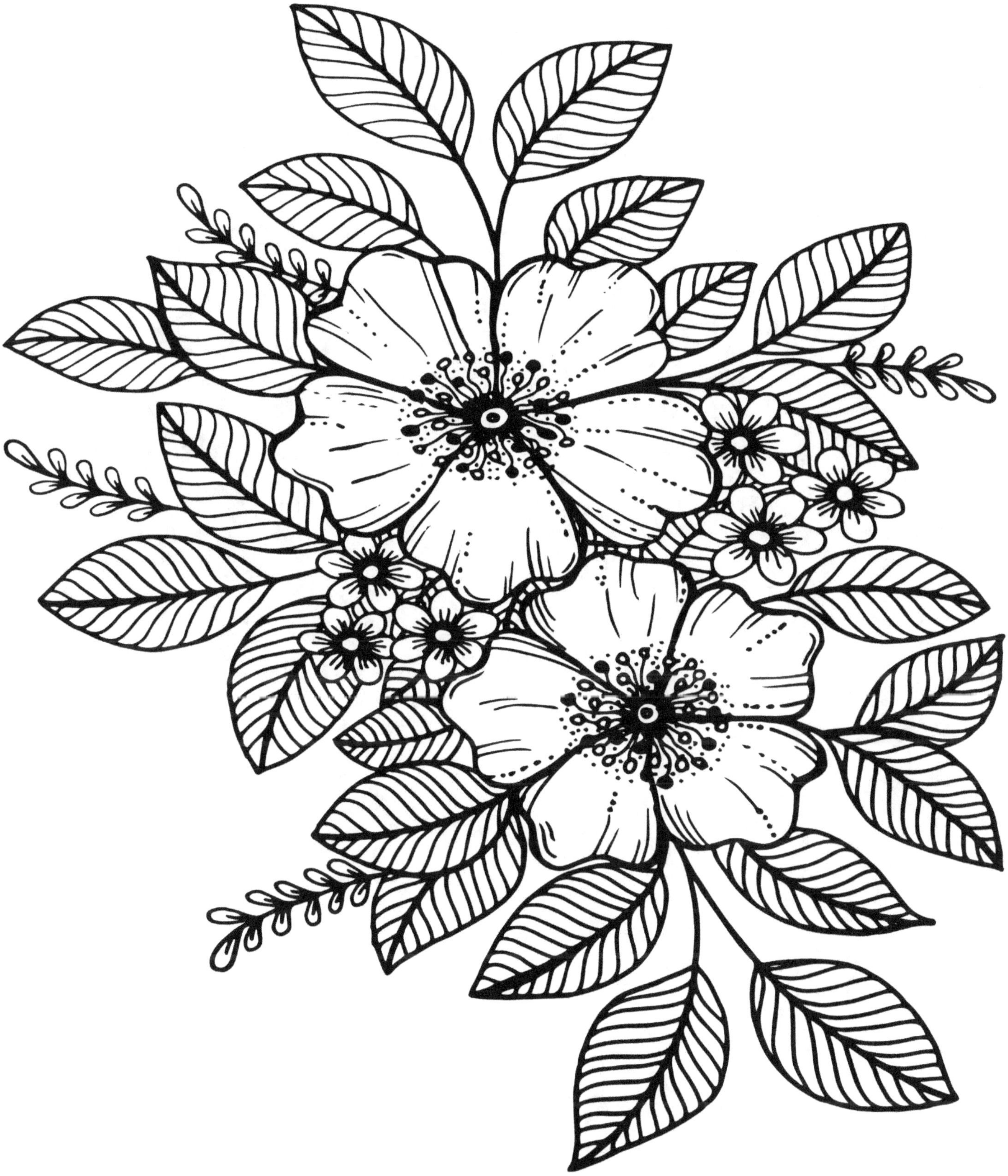

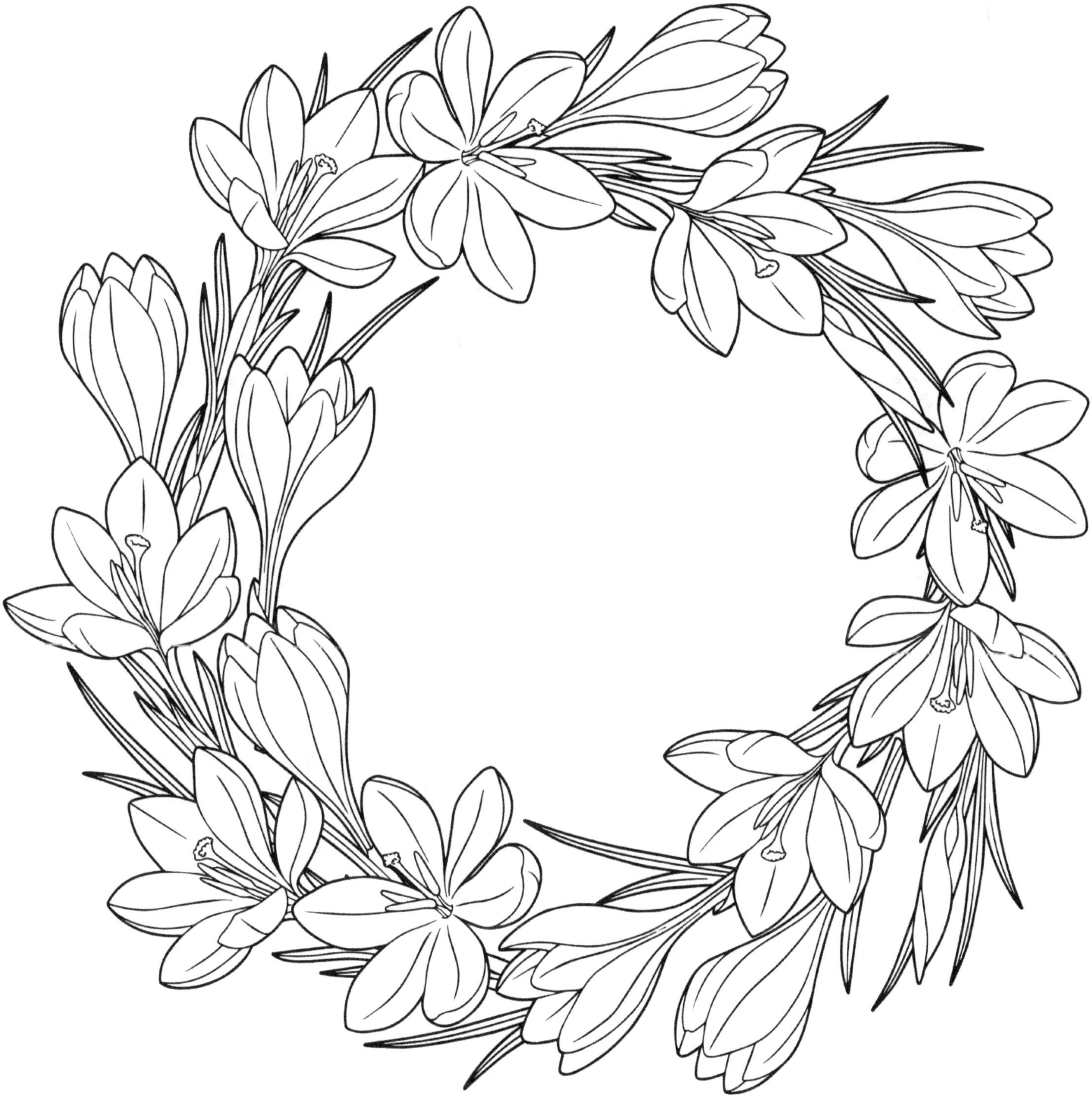

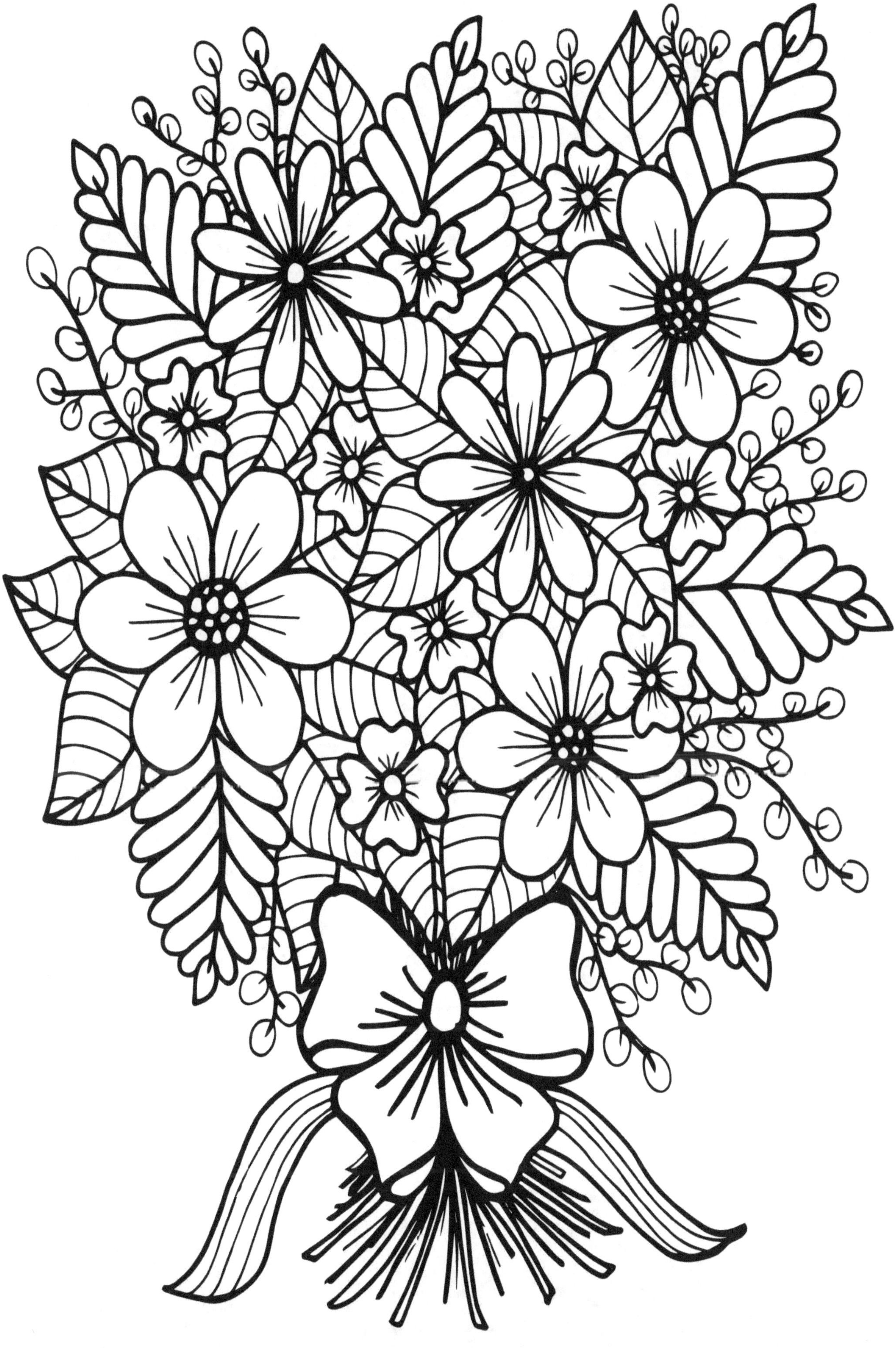

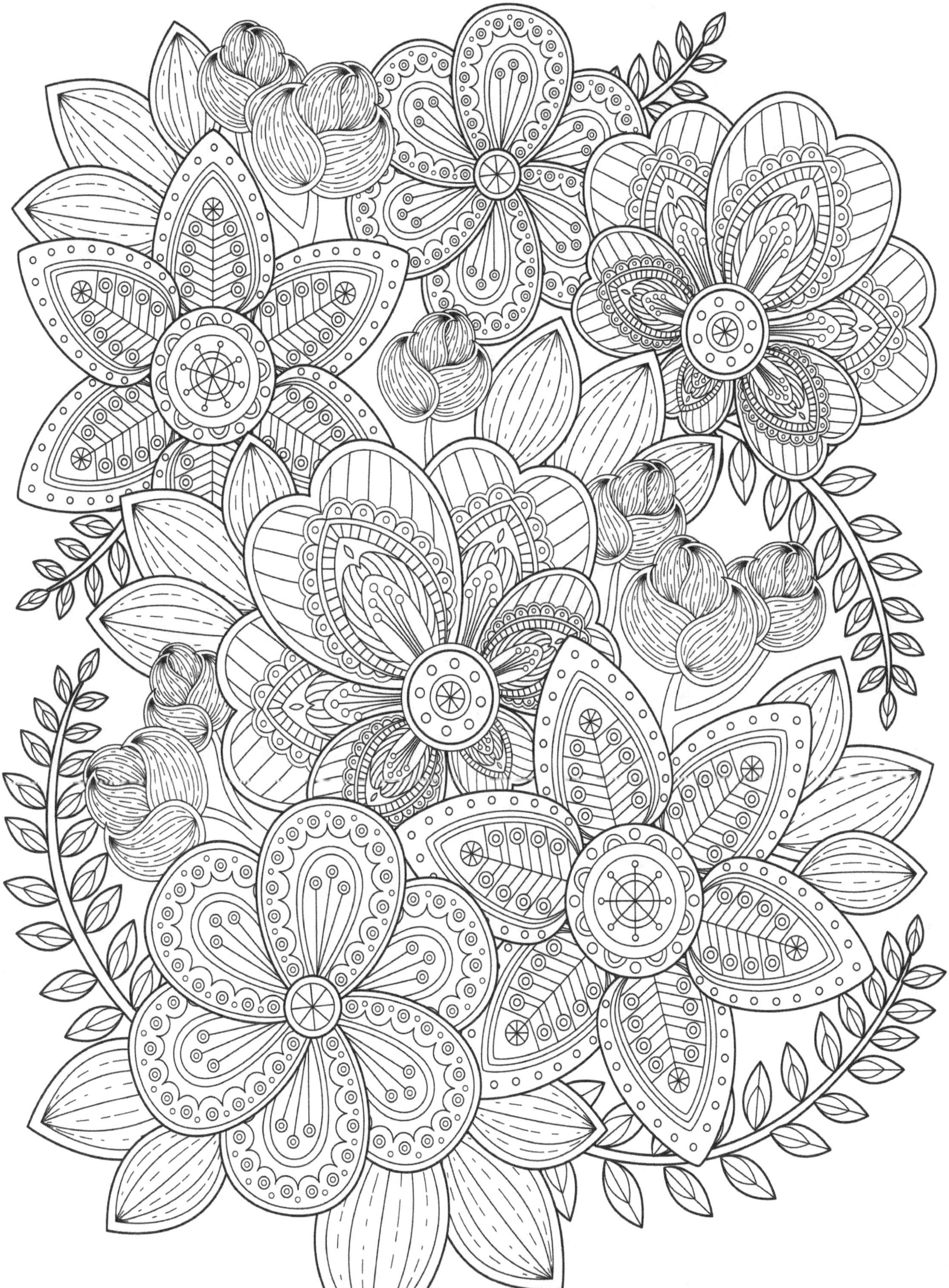

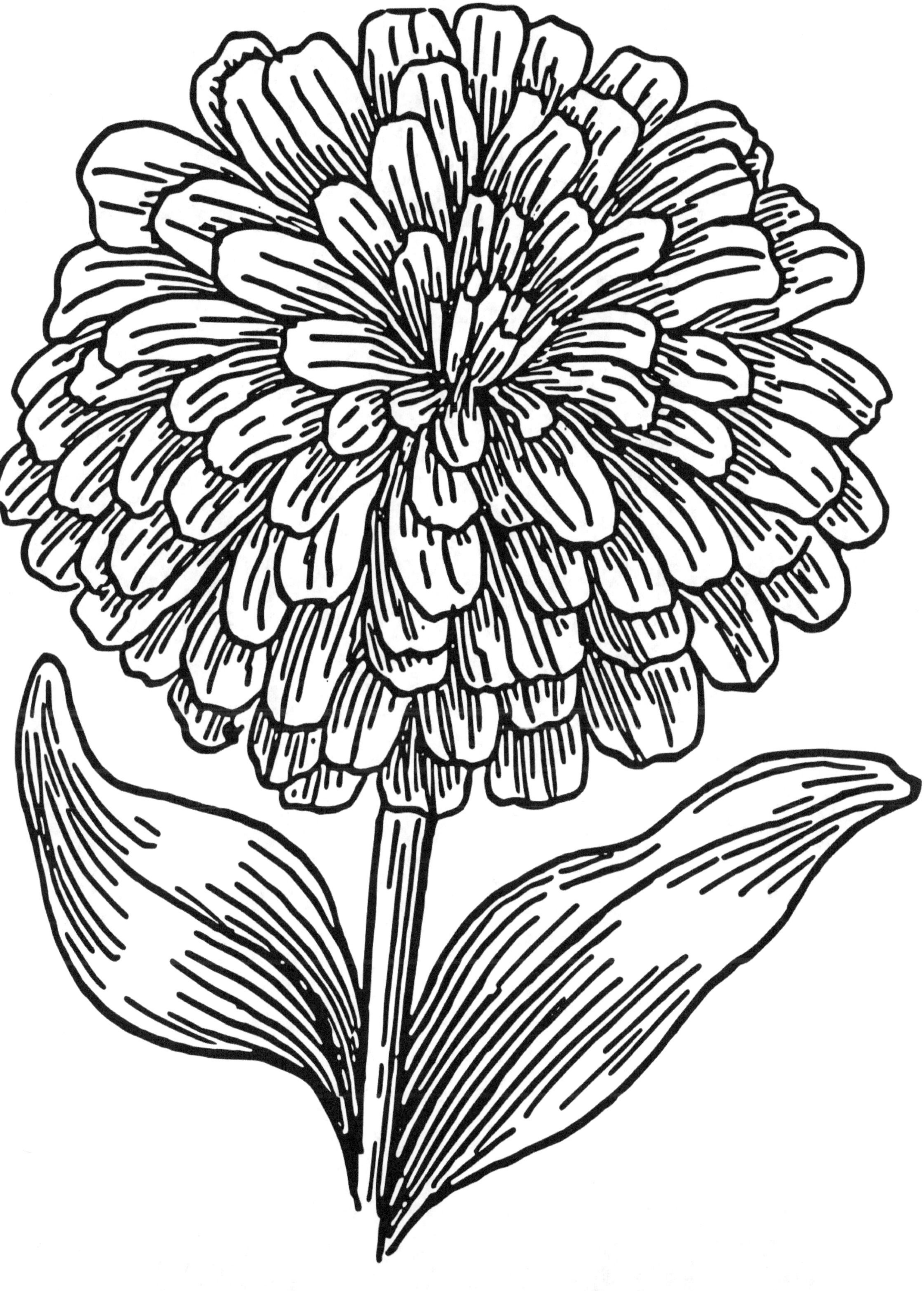

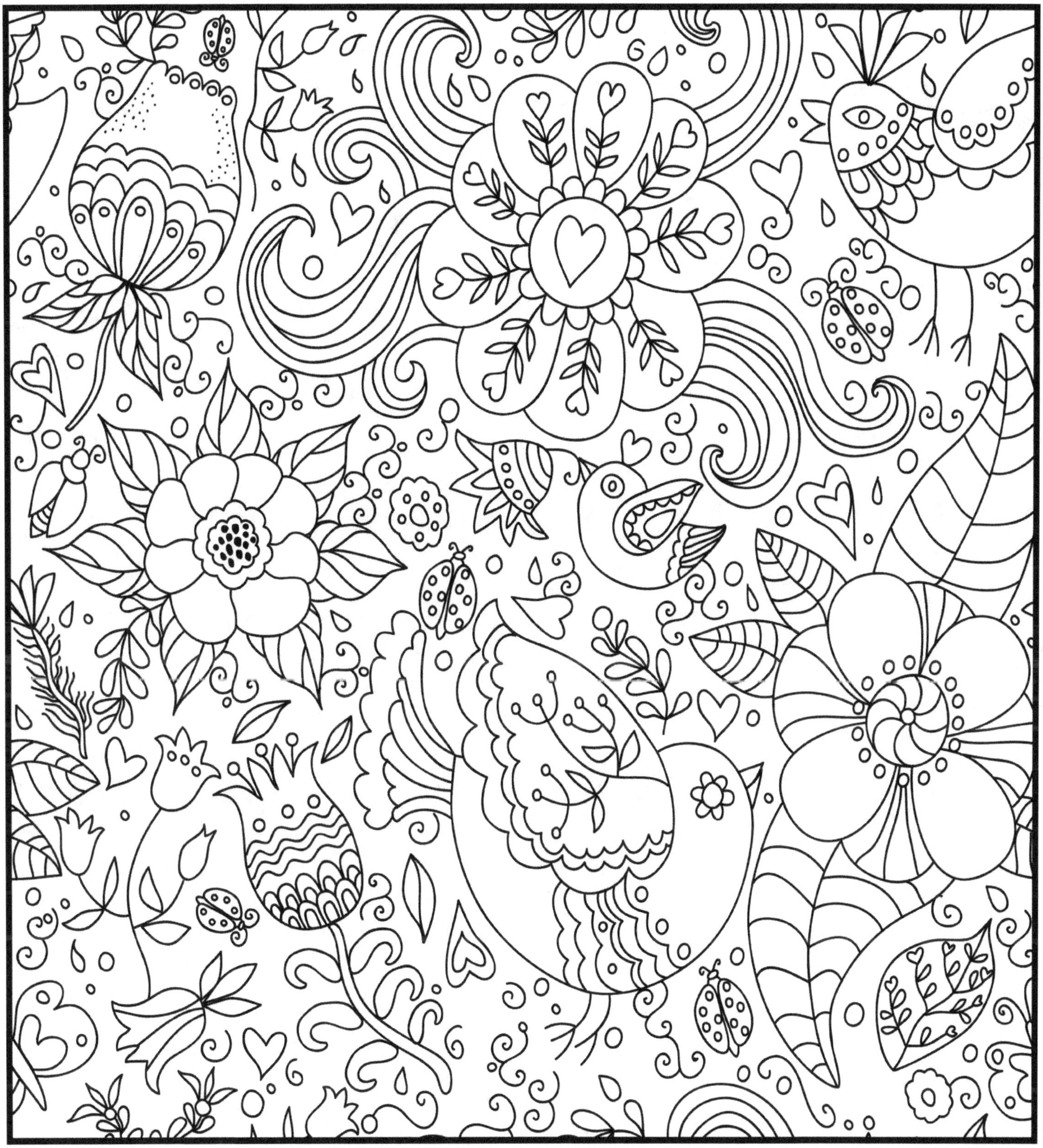

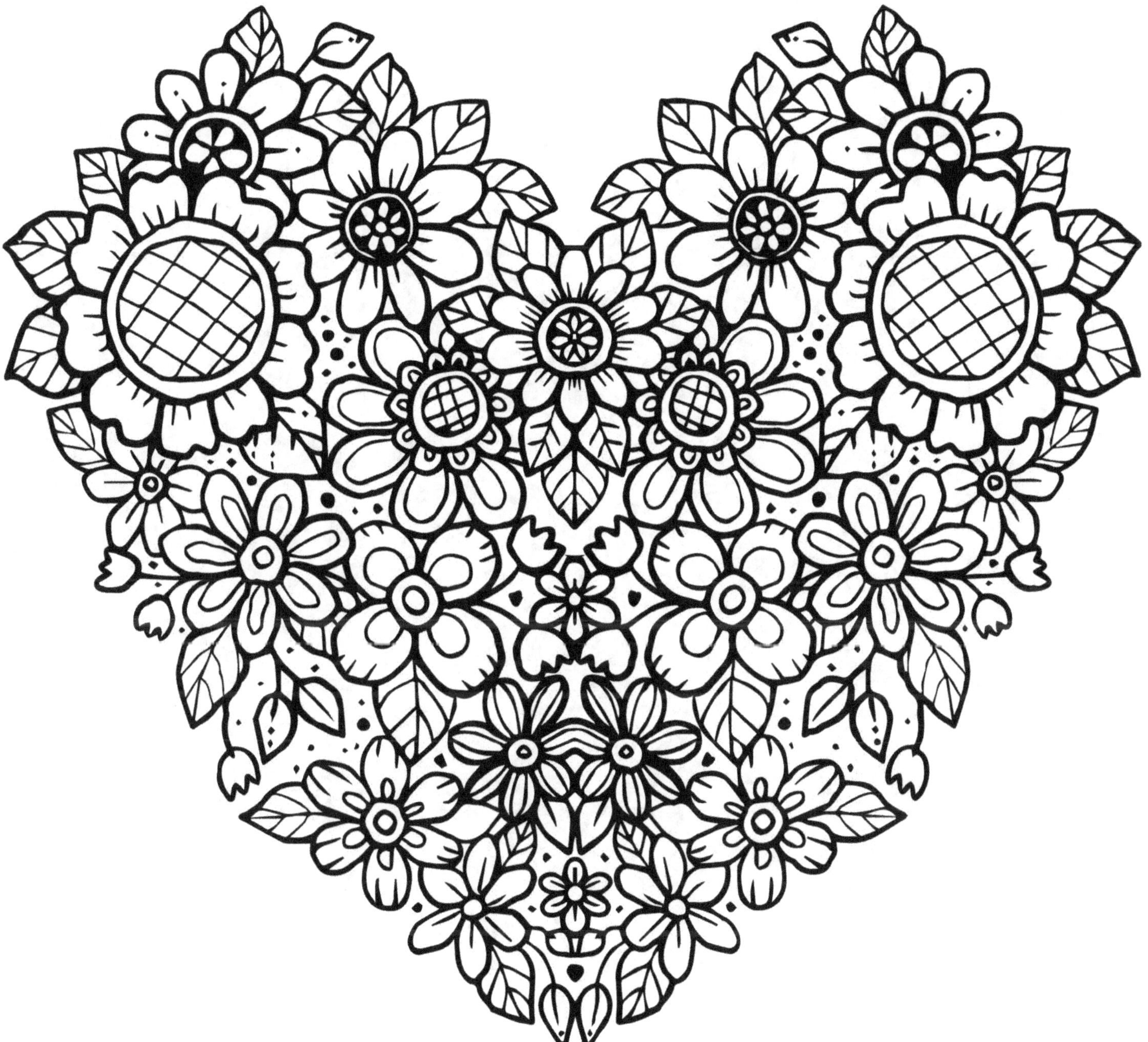

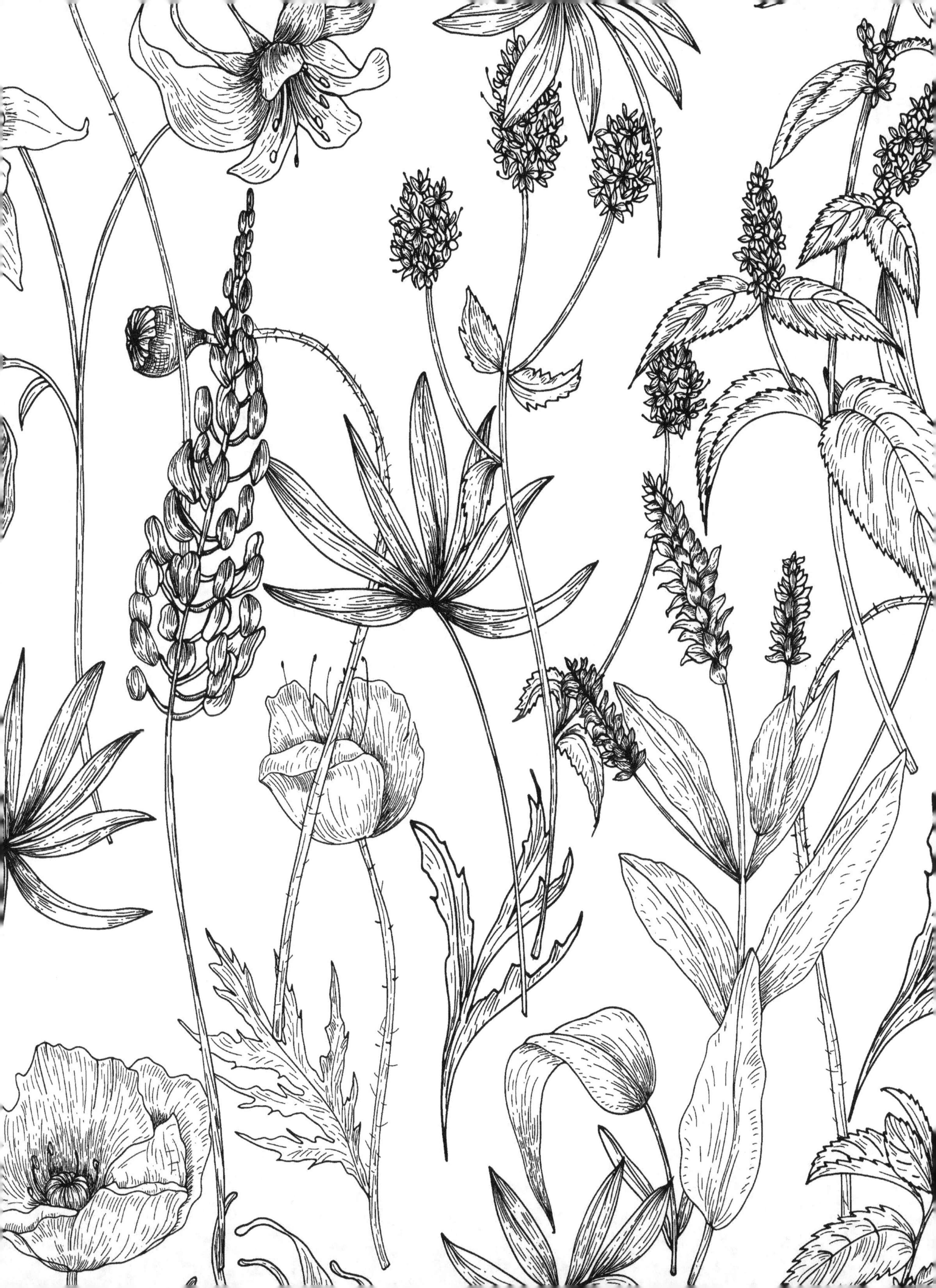

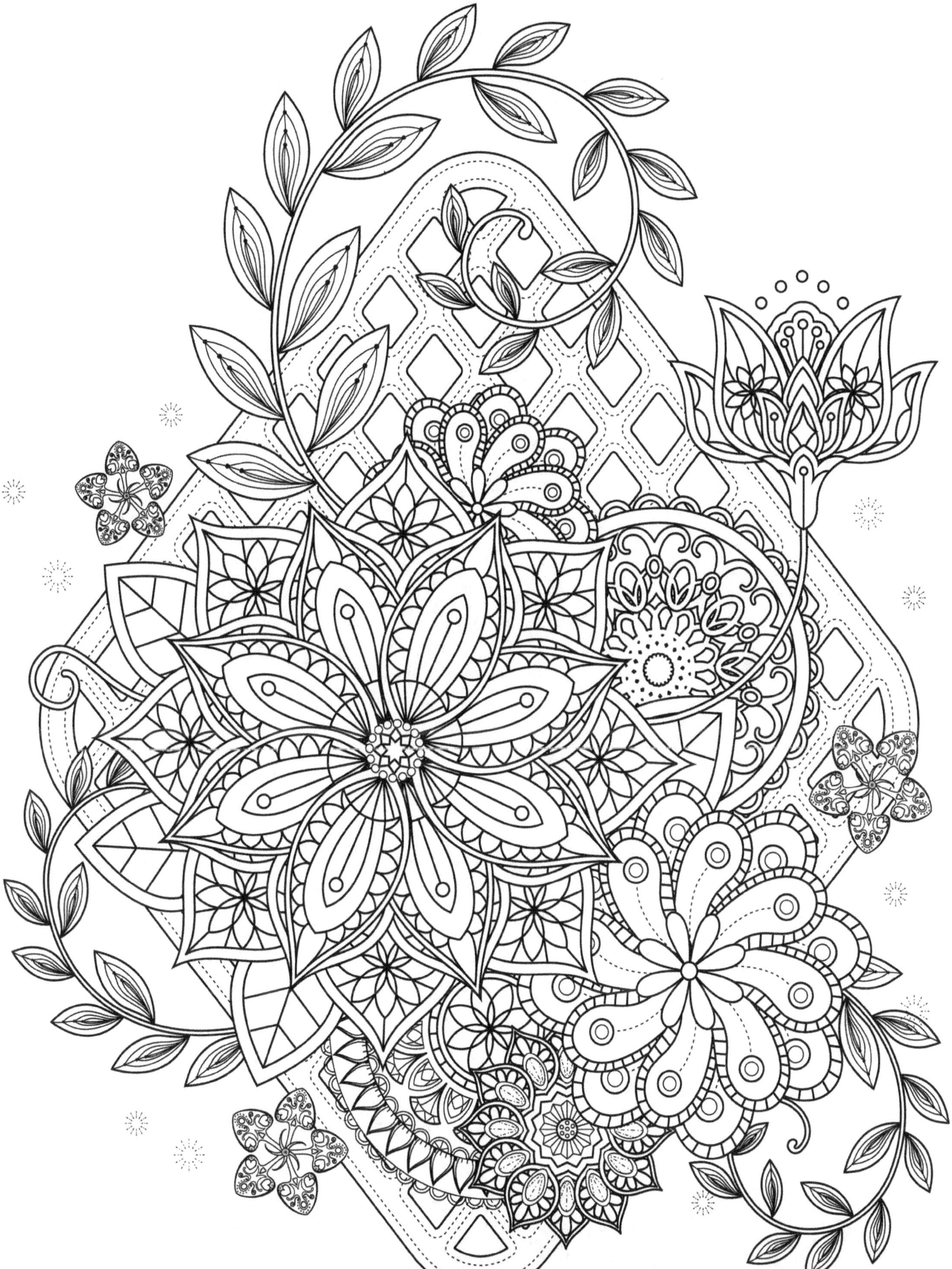

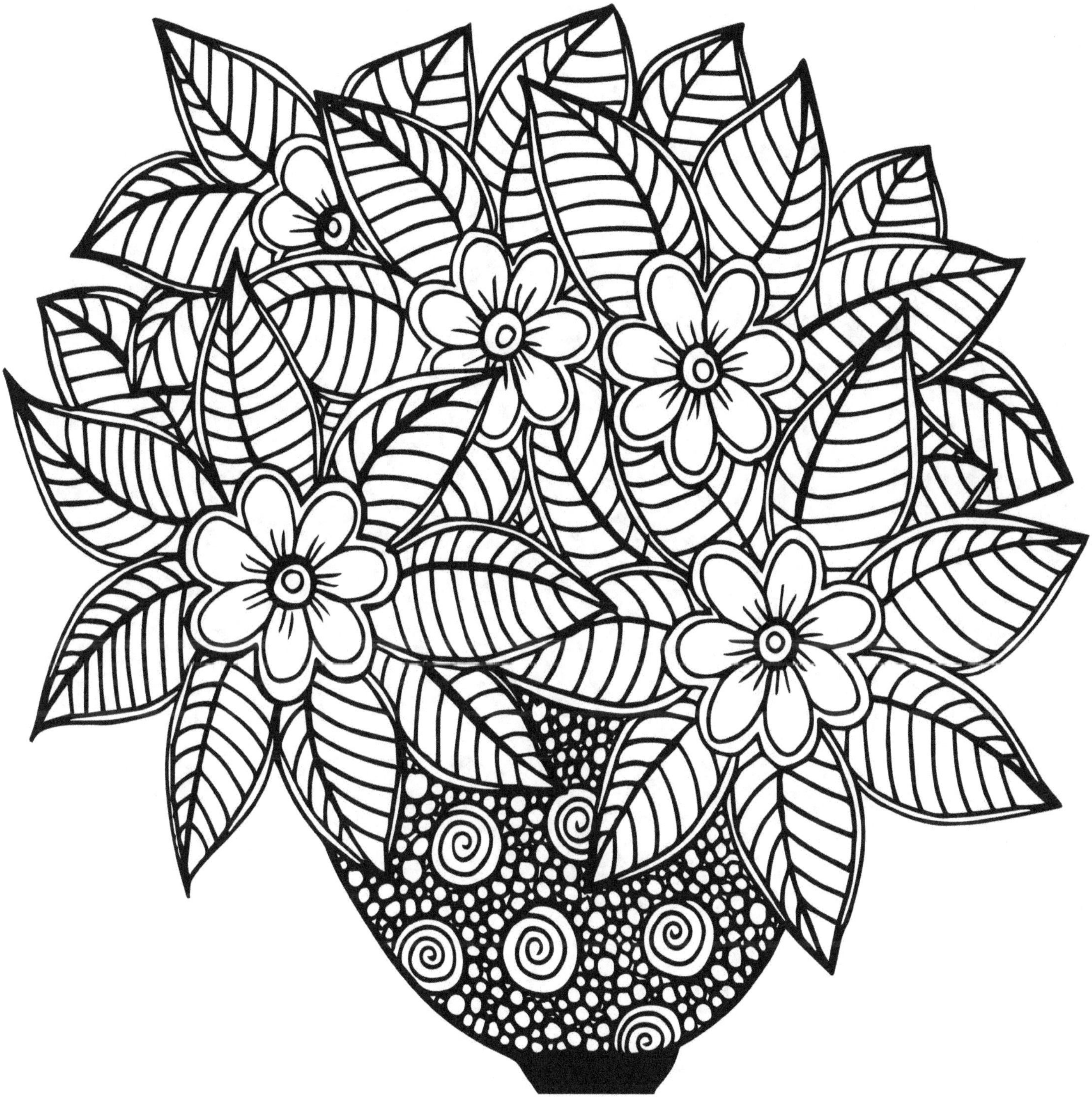

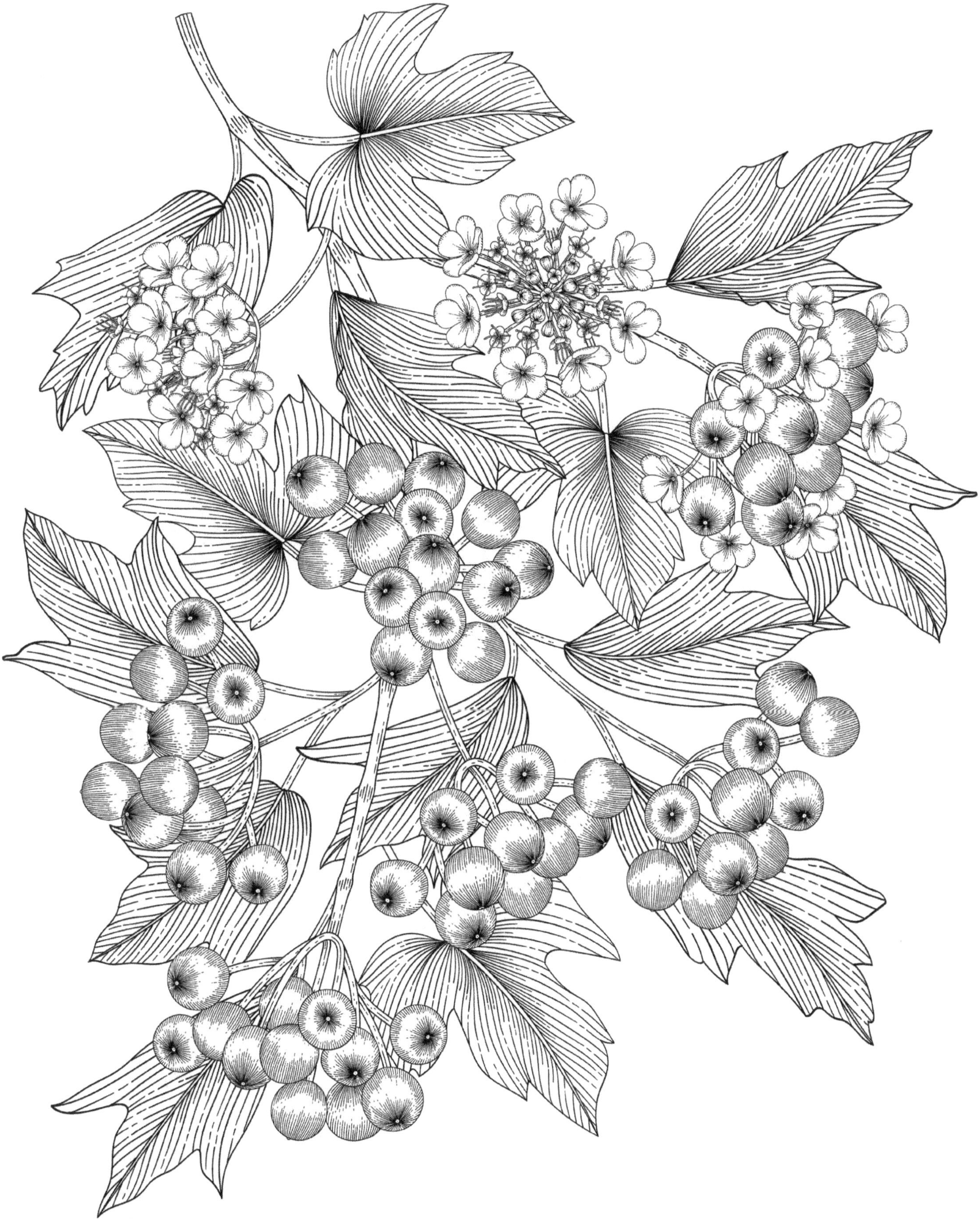

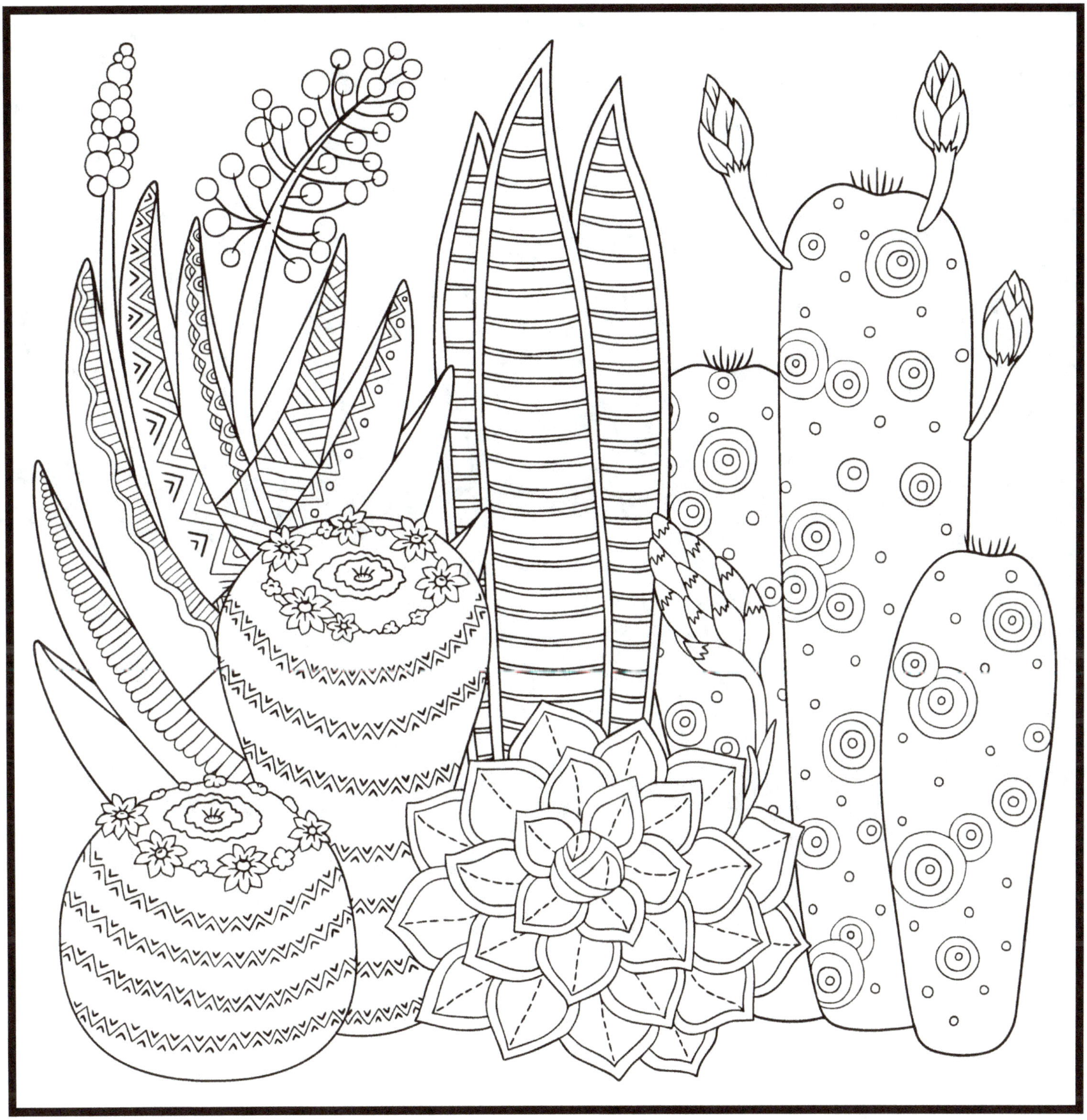

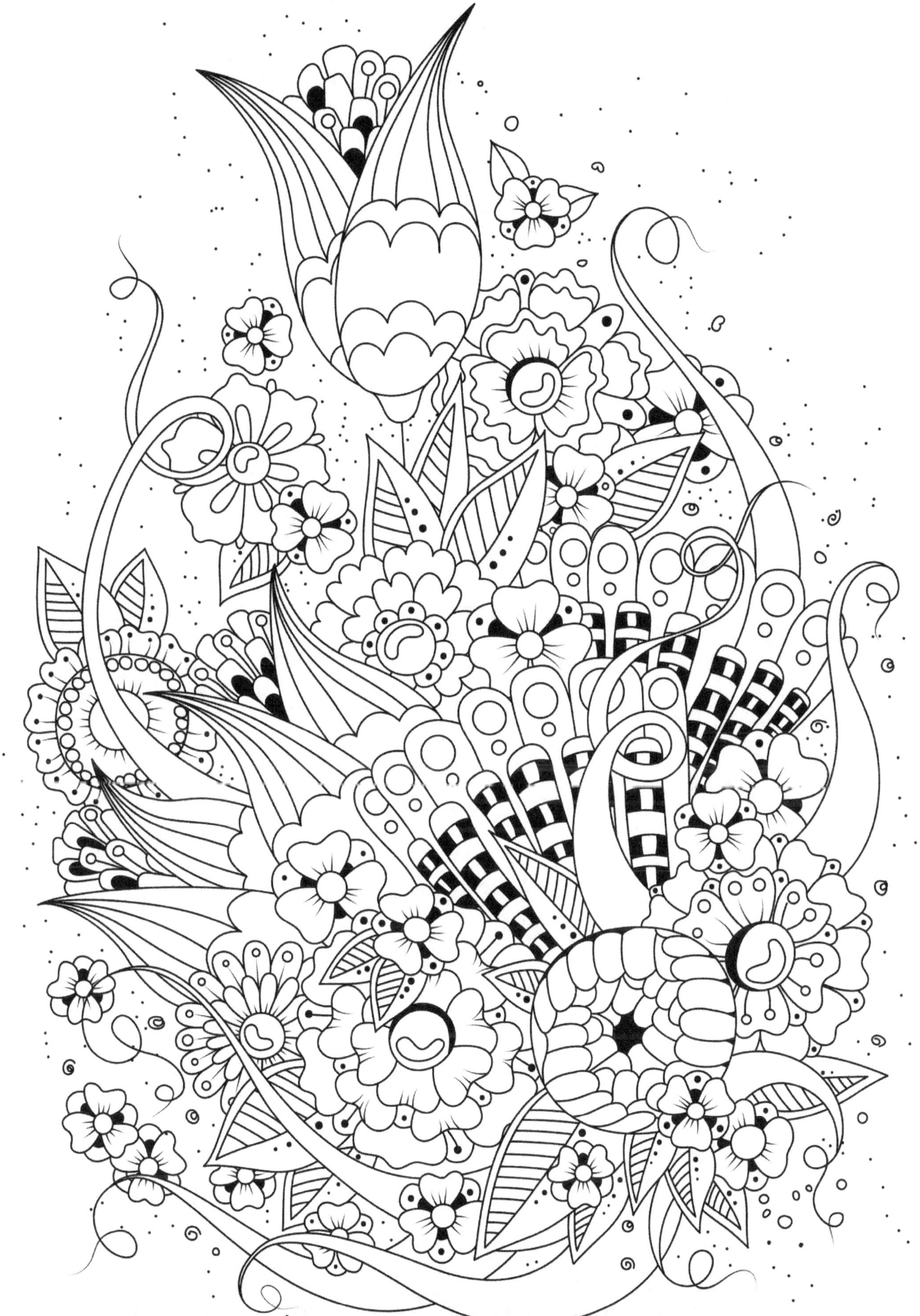

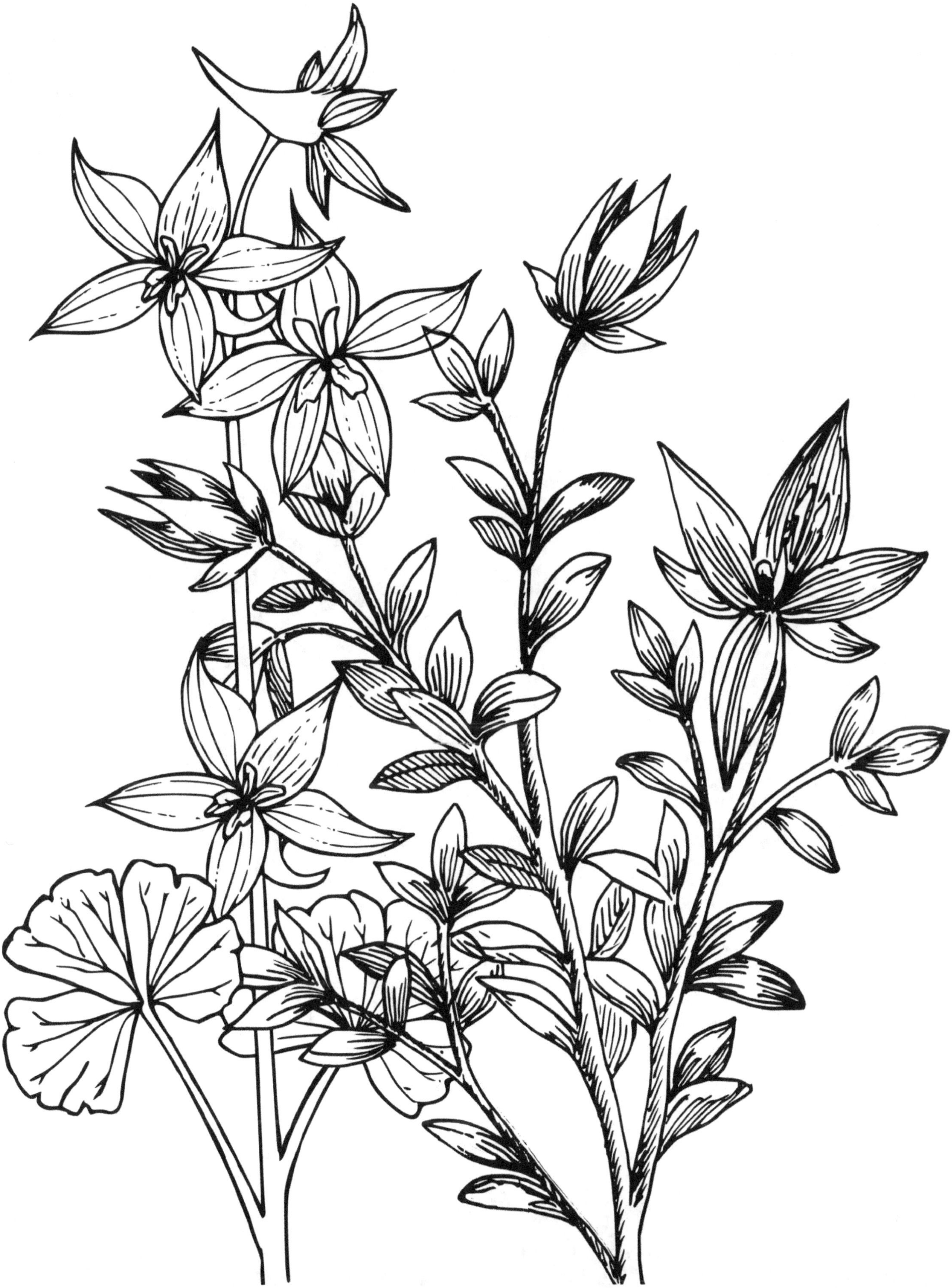

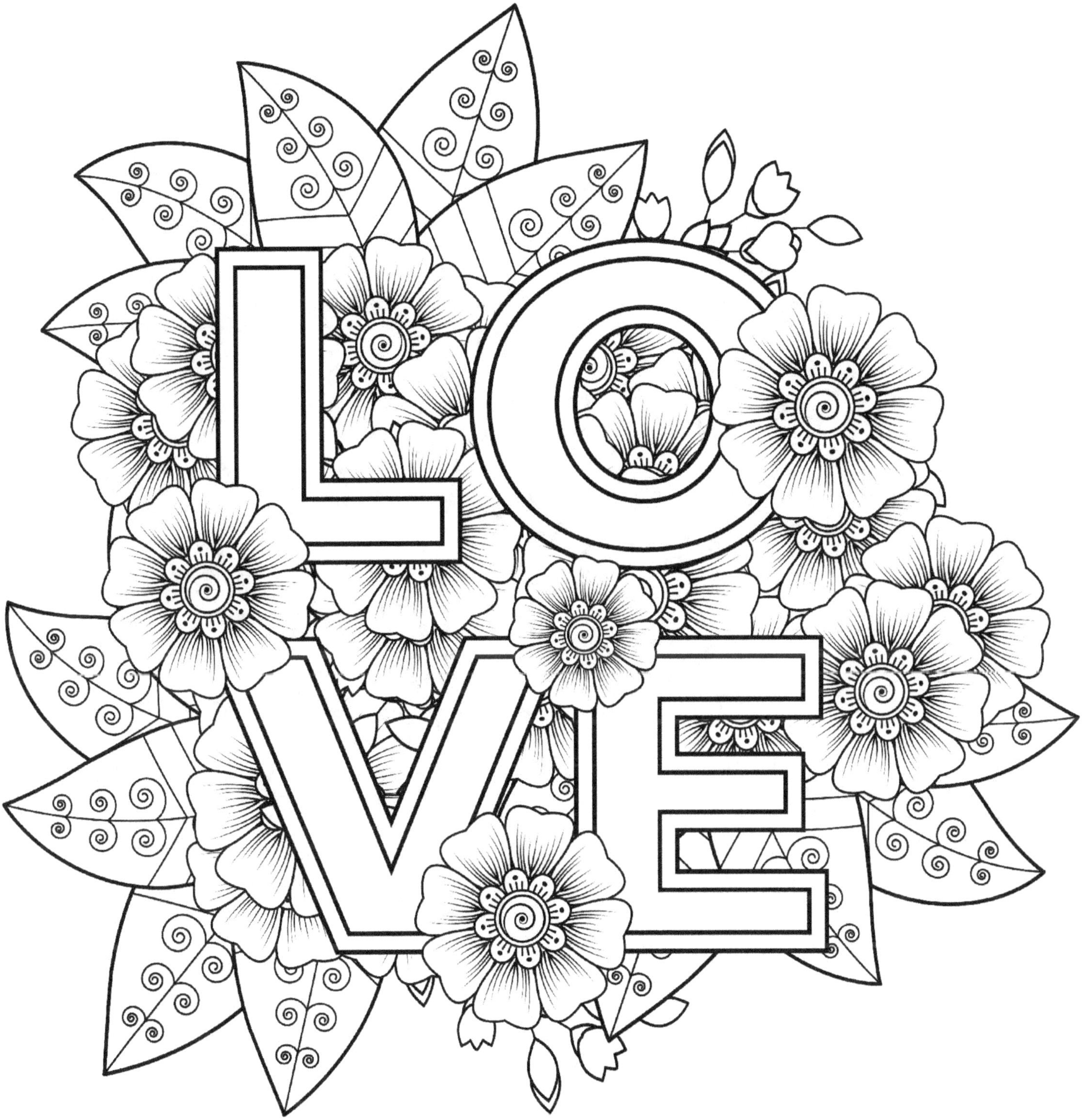
LOVE

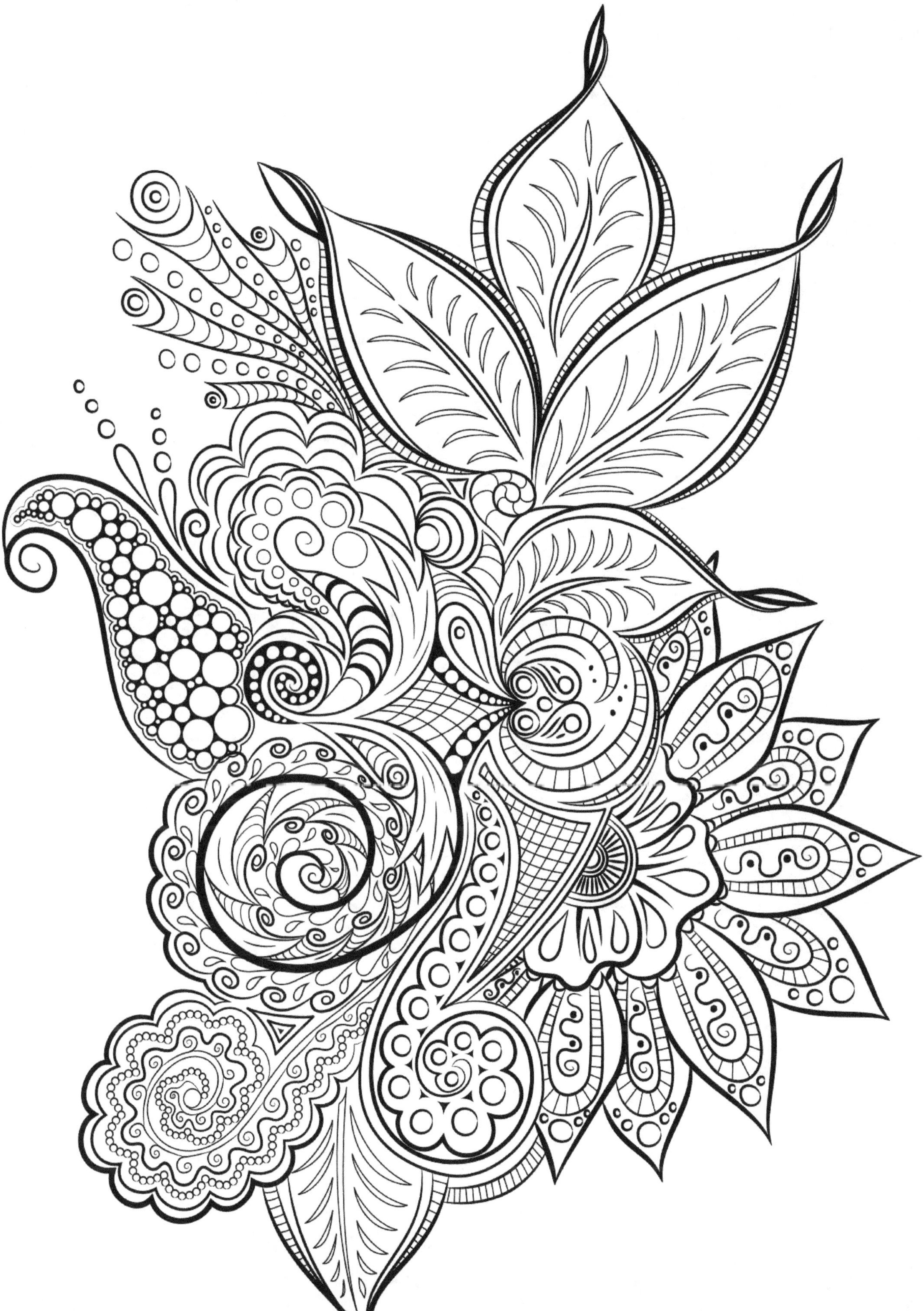

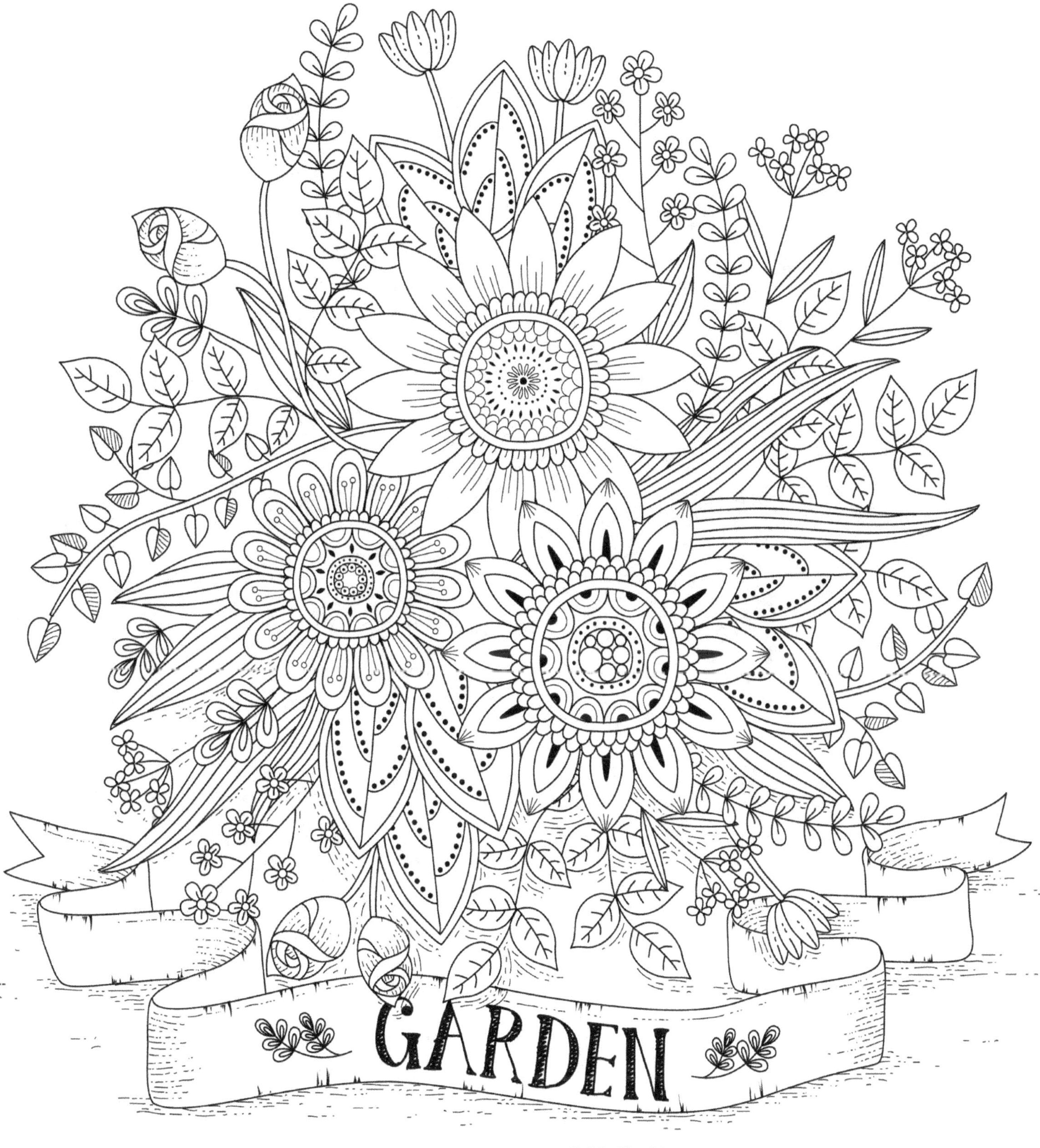
GARDEN

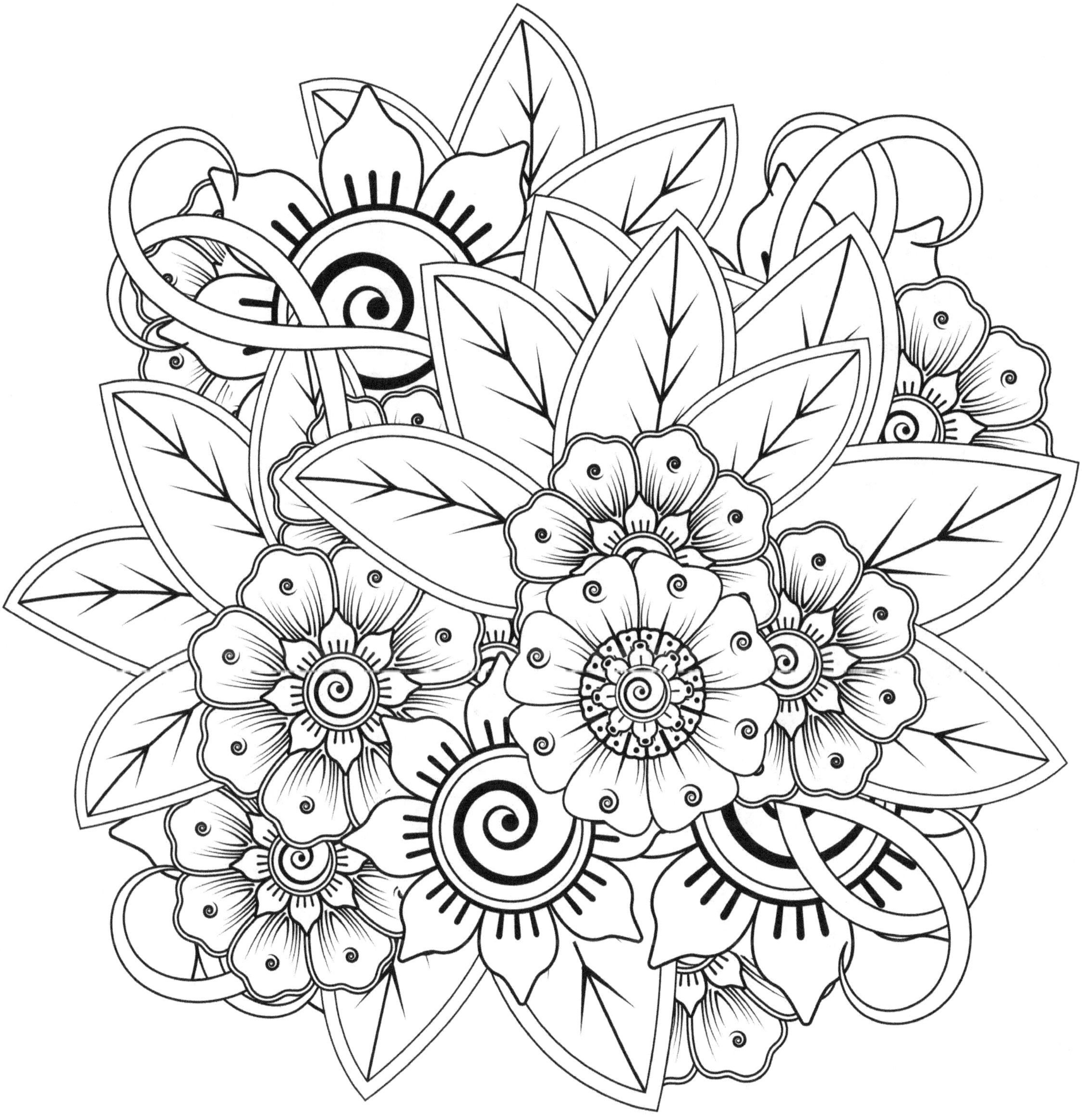

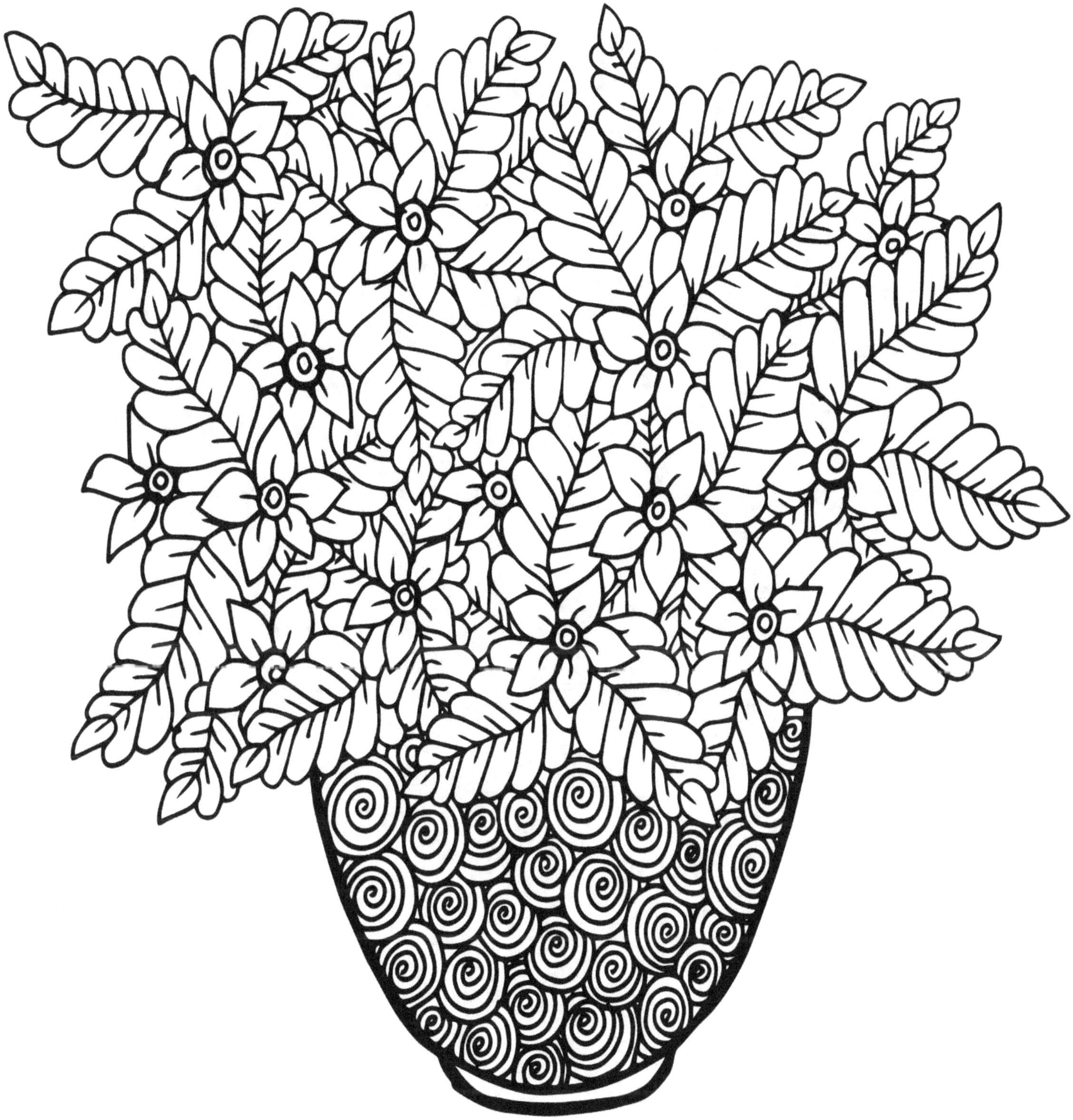

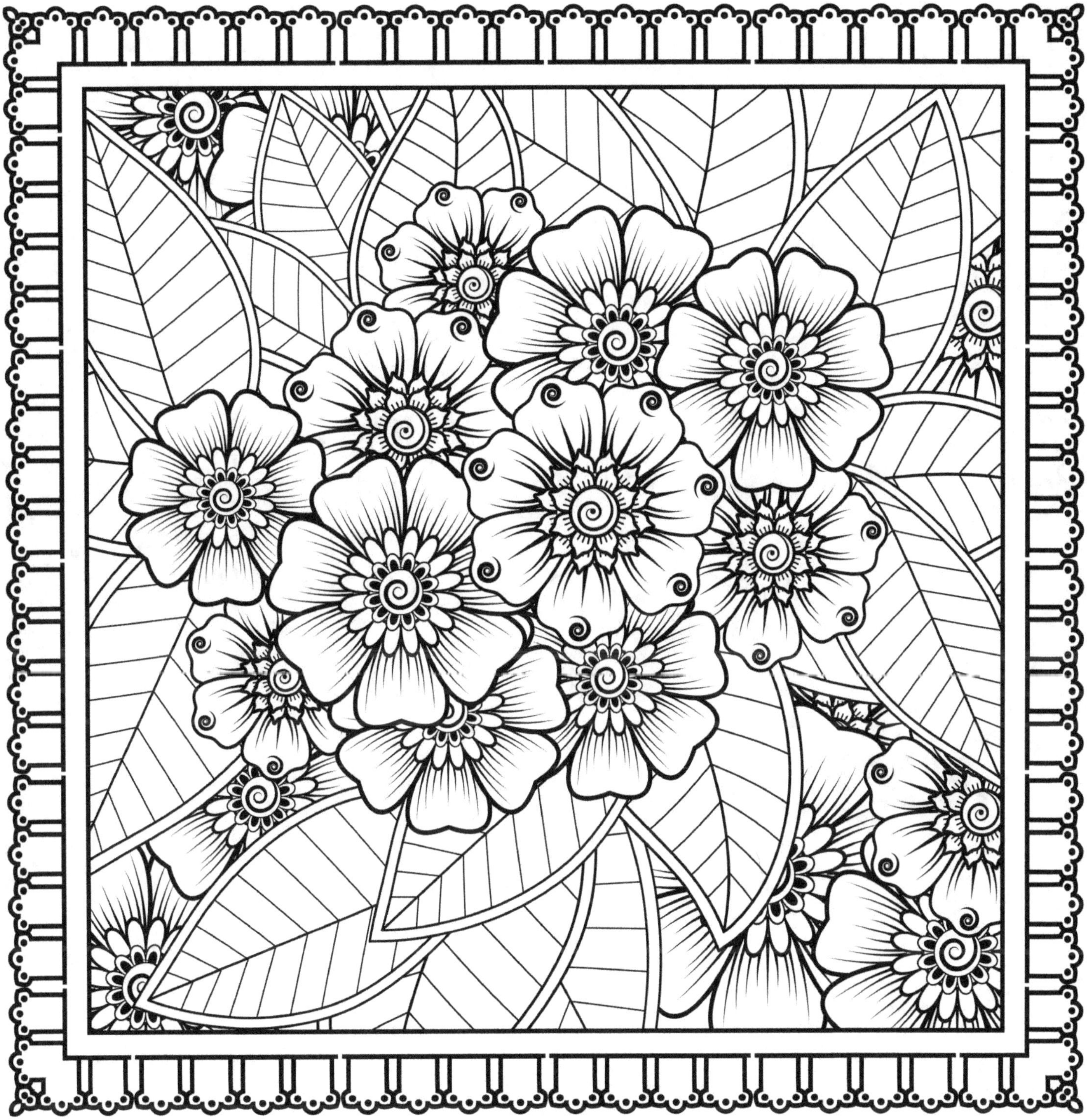

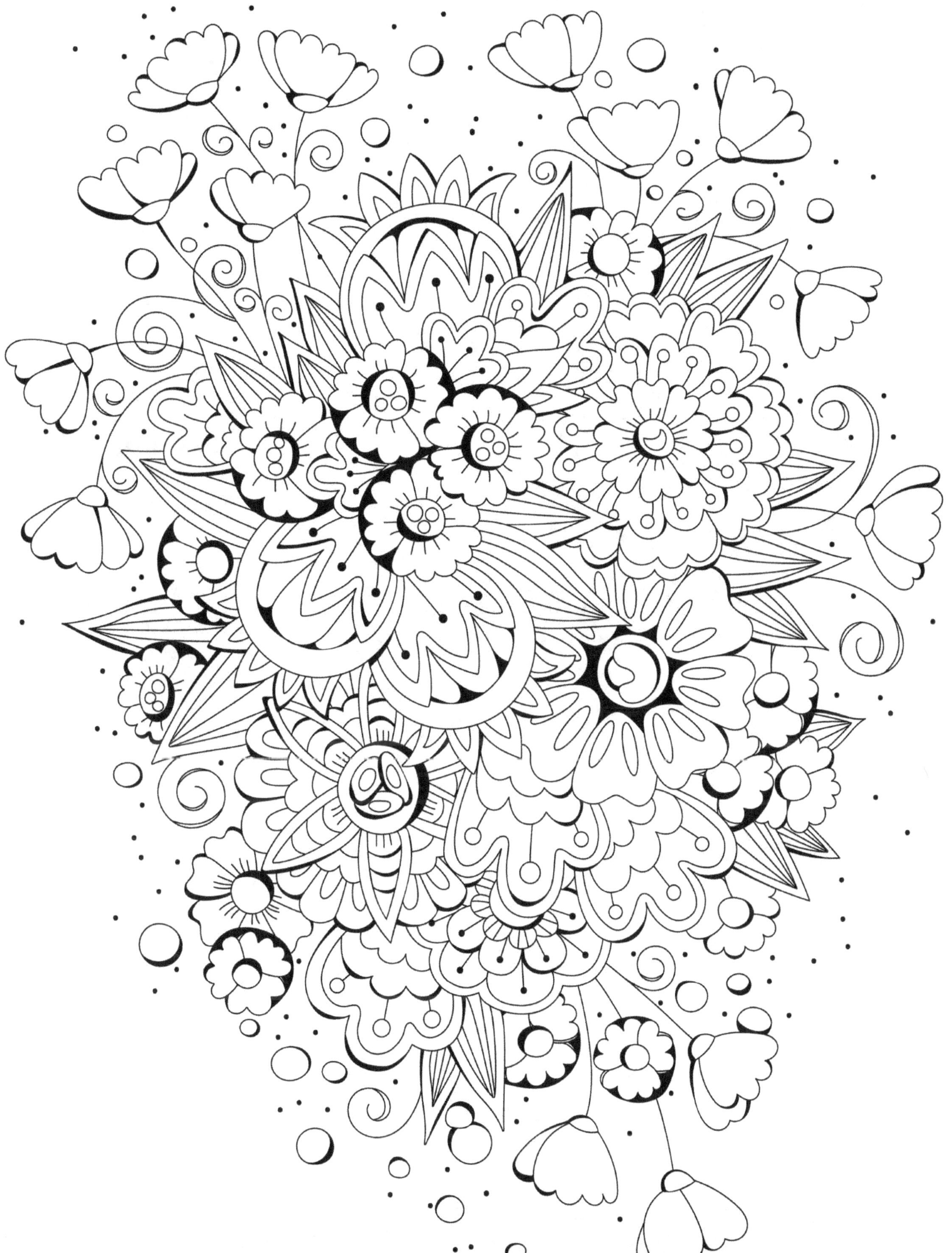

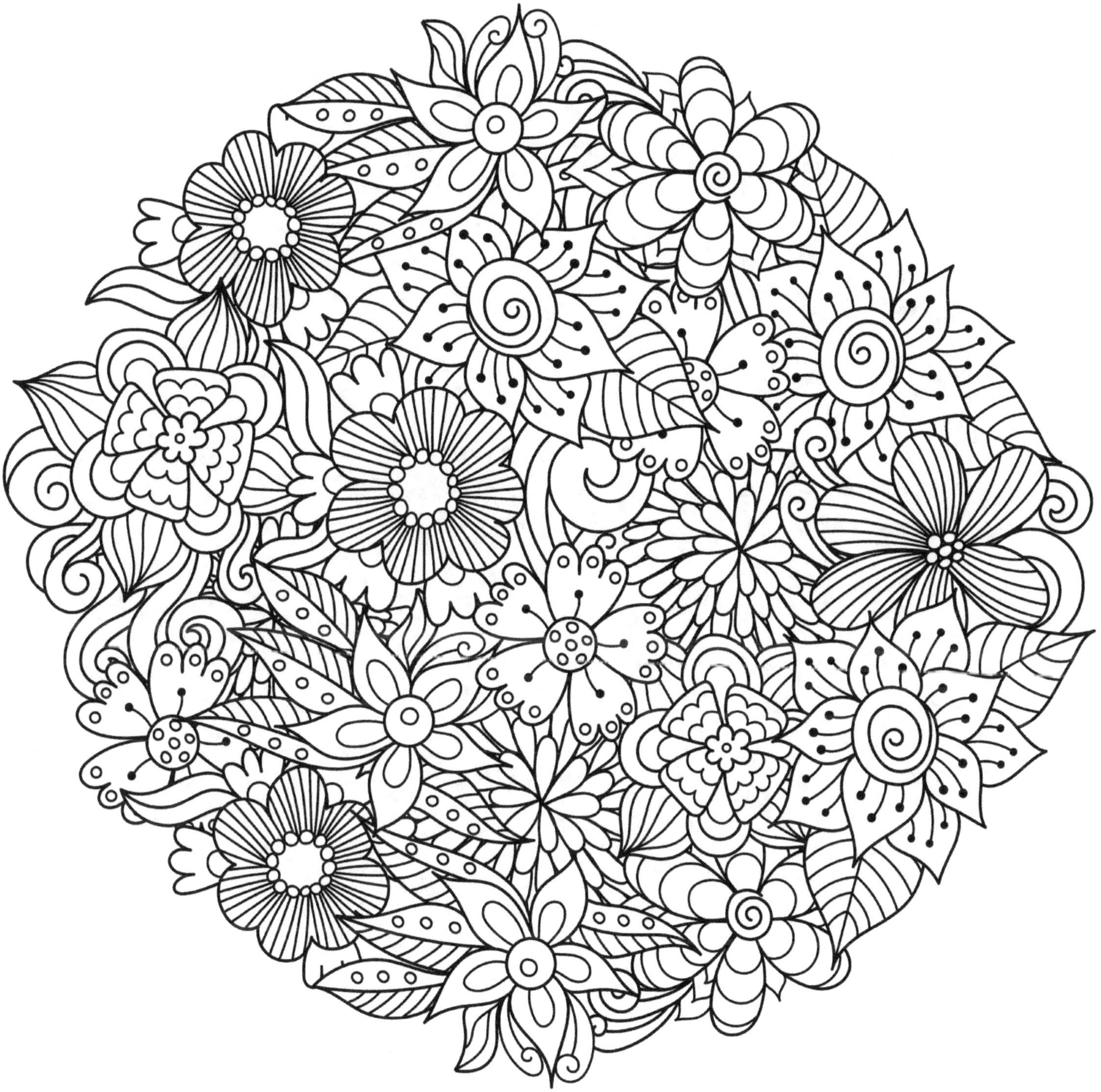

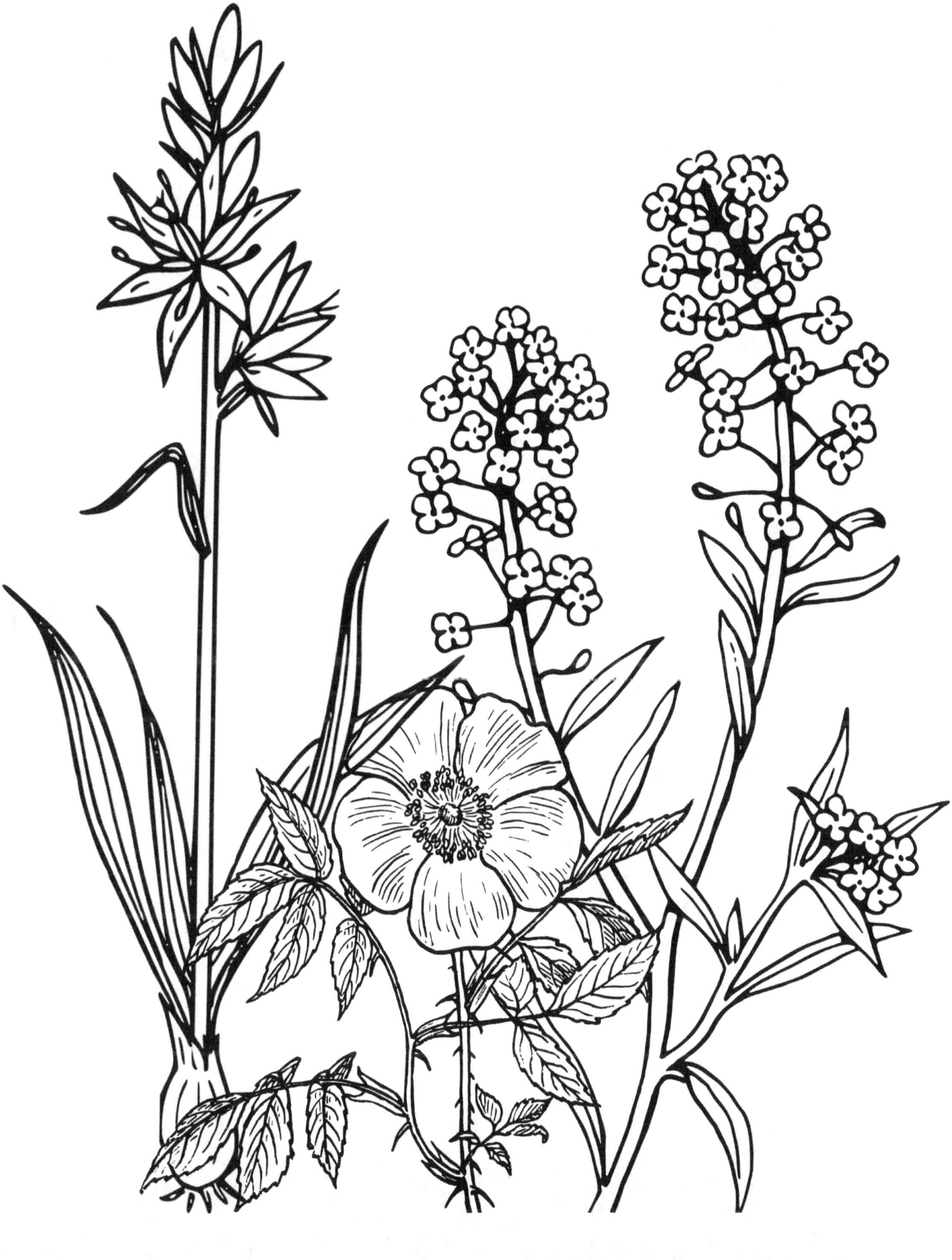

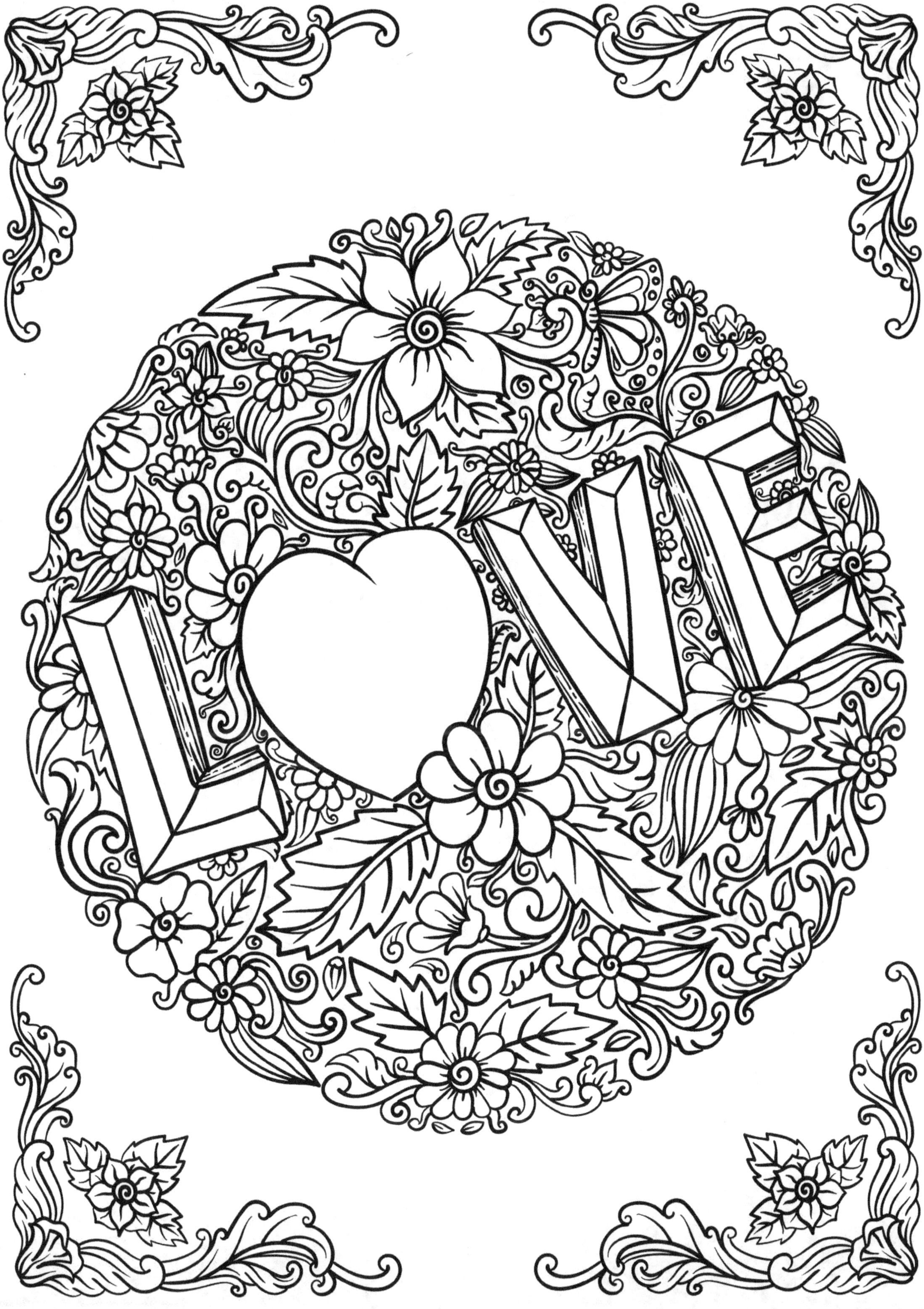
LOVE

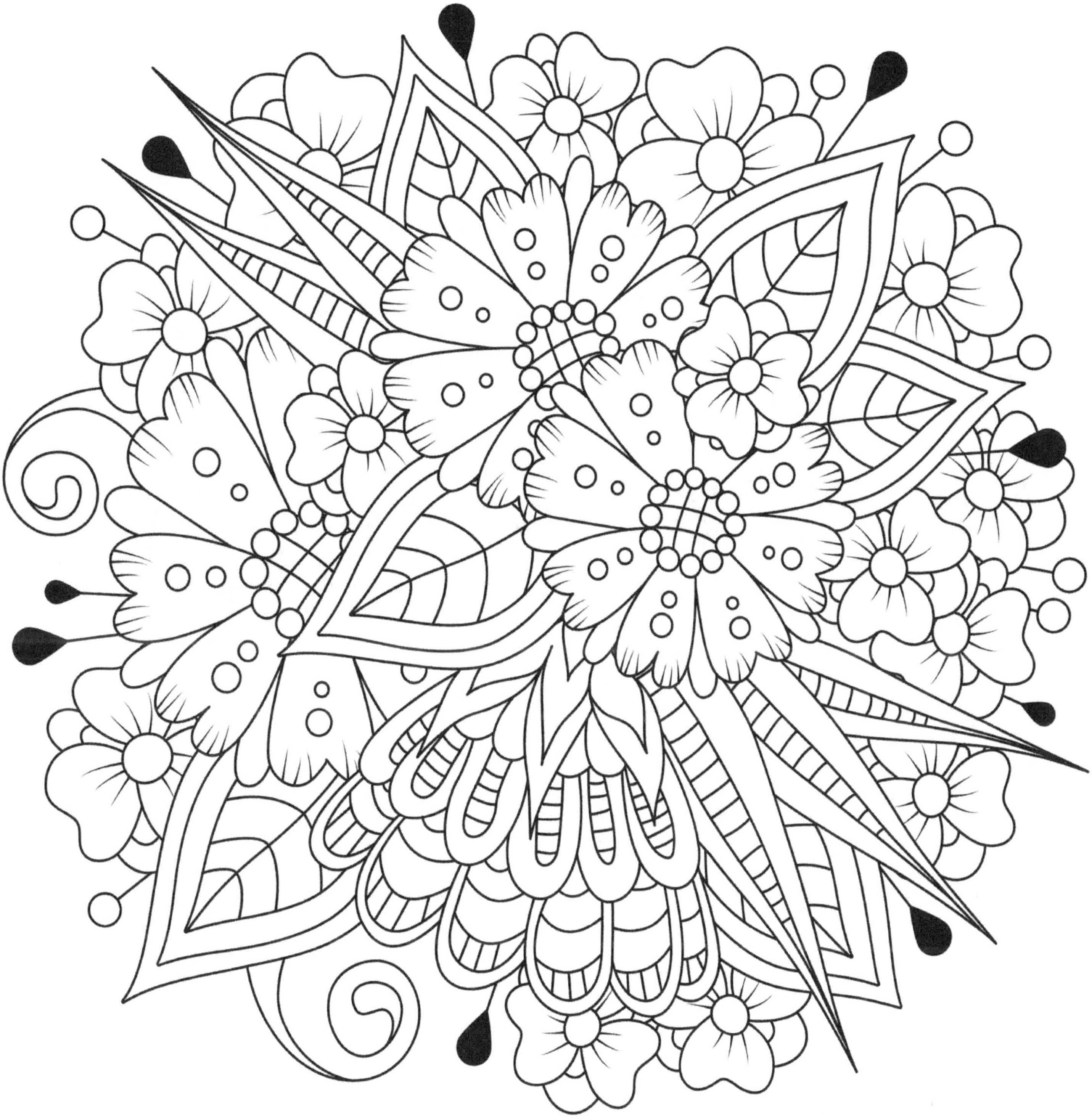

www.ingramcontent.com/pod-product-compliance
Lightning Source LLC
Chambersburg PA
CBHW080457220526
45465CB00006B/2303